I can say with Amos, **"I was no prophet, but a shepherd. And the Lord took me as I followed the flock, and the Lord said to me, Go, prophesy to my people"** (Amos 7:14,15).

David Wilkerson

Joel to "Blow the trumpet in Zion, and sound an alarm in my holy mountain: let all the inhabitants of the land tremble: for the day of the Lord cometh for it is nigh at hand; a day of darkness and of gloominess." Then he urges us on to Joel 2:12, 13 "Therefore also now, saith the Lord, turn ye even to me with all your heart, and with fasting, and with weeping, and mourning, and rend your heart, and not your garments, and turn unto the Lord your God: for he is gracious and merciful, slow to anger, and of great kindness, and repenteth him of the evil."

God grant us the Spirit of obedience to do this, in order that Joel 2:30 may be our experience: "I will shew wonders in the heavens and in the earth." A divine intervention is our only hope.

This trumpet gives no uncertain sound.

Leonard Ravenhill

(Author–"Why Revival Tarries")

Table of Contents

©1985 by
World Challenge, Inc.
P. O. Box 260
Lindale, Texas 75771

Introduction

Dr. Wiersbe has given us a lovely book on walking with the giants. Brother David has given us something better than that in this wonderful book, and it is walking with the prophets.

There is probably no preacher in the nation who is more intimate and knowledgeable on the crime and accelerated depravity in the inner cities of our nation, but he skillfully avoids any horrendous statistics on these youth-crippling vices, which is the result of the anemic preaching of the Word of the living God. There is so little preaching of Christ, repentance, and judgment of sin.

Often I am asked, Is David Wilkerson a prophet? Well, not in the classification of the Old Testament, but surely a prophet in the bracket of the New Testament. I claim for him that God has made him a watchman unto our nation. My slight contribution to this book is like a man taking a bucket of fire and adding it to a volcano, for this book certainly is volcanic. The author sees the church of Jesus Christ wounded, raped, and robbed; and he blows God's trumpet to show us the sin and unbelief that caused it.

He has been broken in compassion for the weak and withered testimony of believers today in a world of arrogant heresy and strident cults. I saw him on one occasion stagger into my office, and his lips trembled as he spoke with tears in his eyes, saying, "Len, I hardly dare put on paper and publish what the Lord has given to me." But he has done this, and I for one am tremendously glad that he did.

The book will bring a cry of joy from the young preachers who are asking for a spiritual voice compelling the church back to her original calling of holiness and power. The author has followed the command of

Chapter 1
The Destruction of America

"Behold, the name of the Lord cometh from far, burning with his anger, and the burden thereof is heavy: his lips are full of indignation, and his tongue as a devouring fire. And the Lord shall cause his glorious voice to be heard, and shall shew the lighting down of his arm, with the indignation of his anger, and with the flame of a devouring fire, with scattering, and tempest, and hailstones" (Isaiah 30:27,30).

"Yea, the stork in the heaven knoweth her appointed times; and the turtle and the crane and the swallow observe the time of their coming; but my people know not the judgment of the Lord" (Jeremiah 8:7).

America is going to be destroyed by fire! Sudden destruction is coming and few will escape. Unexpectedly, and in one hour, a hydrogen holocaust will engulf America—and this nation will be no more.

It is because America has sinned against the greatest light. Other nations are just as sinful, but none are as flooded with gospel light as ours. God is going to judge America for its violence, its crimes, its backslidings, its murdering of millions of babies, its flaunting of homosexuality and sadomasochism, its corruption, its drunkenness and drug abuse, its form of godliness without power, its lukewarmness toward Christ, its rampant divorce and adultery, its lewd pornography, its child molestations, its cheatings, its robbings, its dirty movies, and its occult practices.

In one hour it will all be over. To the natural mind it is insanity to come against a prosperous, powerful nation and cry out, "It's all over! Judgment is at the door! Our days are numbered!" The church is asleep, the congregations are at ease, and the shepherds slumber. How they will scoff and laugh at this message. Theologians will reject it because they can't fit it into their doctrine. The pillow prophets of peace and prosperity will publicly denounce it.

I no longer care. God has made my face like flint and put steel in my backbone. I am blowing the Lord's trumpet with all my might. Let the whole world and all the church call me crazy, but I must blow the trumpet and awaken God's people. Believe it or not, America is about to be shaken and set aside by swift and horrible judgments. Many other praying believers who have been shut in with God are hearing the very same message—"Judgment is at the door! Prepare, awaken!"

Ever since this message came to me, I have been searching God's Word from cover to cover. No prophecy is valid unless it is positively confirmed by God's holy Word. I discovered in the Word God's pattern of judgment. Although it is true He will never again destroy the earth by flood, He does use fire. All the prophets predicted judgment by fire on nations and peoples who forsook God and became hopelessly wicked. Their prophecies were dual, directed to their generation in which they prophesied and also to future generations who committed the same crimes against God. Prophecies against Babylon and Israel were fulfilled to the letter. But many of these prophecies also refer to the "latter days," to those who live at the end of the ages. Paul said, "Now all these things happened unto them for ensamples: and they are written for our admonition, upon whom the ends of the world are come" (1 Corinthians 10:11).

Perhaps only the overcomers will accept and hear the sound of this trumpet blast, but I proceed with these warnings because God called me to be a watchman. I hear the Word of God to Ezekiel ringing in my ears, "Son of man, speak to the children of thy people, and say unto them, When I bring the sword upon a land, if the people of the land take a man of their coasts, and set him for their watchman: If when he seeth the sword come upon the land, he blow the trumpet, and warn the people; Then whosoever heareth the sound of the trumpet, and taketh not warning; if the sword come, and take him away, his blood shall be upon his own head. He heard the sound of the trumpet, and took not warning; his blood shall be upon him. But he that taketh warning shall deliver his soul. But if the watchman see the sword come, and blow not the trumpet, and the people be not warned; if the sword come, and take any person from among them, he is taken away in his iniquity; but his blood will I require at the watchman's hand. So thou, O son of man, I have set thee a watchman unto the house of Israel; therefore thou shalt hear the word at my mouth, and warn them from me" (Ezekiel 33:2-7).

America Is Modern Babylon

I believe modern Babylon is present-day America, including its corrupt society and its whorish church system. No other nation on earth fits the description in Revelation 18 but America, the world's biggest fornicator with the merchants of all nations. Ancient Babylon was long destroyed when John received this vision.

John saw fiery destruction coming in one hour. "There-fore shall her plagues come in one day, death, and mourning, and famine; and she shall be utterly burned with fire: for strong is the Lord God who judgeth her. And the kings of the earth, who have committed forni-cation and lived deliciously with her, shall bewail her, and lament for her, when they shall see the smoke of her burning, standing afar off for the fear of her torment, saying, Alas, alas that great city Babylon, that mighty city! for in one hour is thy judgment come" (Revelation 18:8-10).

Just as Israel was called the city of God, America is referred to as Babylon, that mighty city. It is a people, a land. In one hour it is going to be wiped out and con-sumed by fire. Judgment will fall upon the major cit-ies, the towns, with fire consuming what was once a prosperous, thriving, safe, and tranquil land. "And the merchants of the earth shall weep and mourn over her; for no man buyeth their merchandise any more. And the good things thy soul lusted after are departed from thee, and all things which were dainty and goodly are departed from thee, and thou shalt find them no more at all. For in one hour so great riches is come to nothing" (Revelation 18:11,14,17).

The great eagle with great wings is about to fall from its lofty position on the highest branch of all nations. The vine that was planted "in a land of traffic, in a city of merchants, by great waters" is about to die. "It was planted in a good soil by great waters, that it might bring forth branches, and that it might bear fruit, that it might be a goodly vine" (Ezekiel 17:8).

God's prophetic word from Ezekiel to Israel is also God's word for America: "Thus saith the Lord God; Shall it prosper? Shall he not pull up the roots there-of,...that it wither? It shall wither in all the leaves of her spring, even without great power or many people to pluck it up by the roots thereof....Shall it not utterly wither, when the east wind toucheth it?" (Ezekiel 17:9,10).

Oh, what horrible and swift judgments are just ahead, very imminent, upon this nation that has cast aside holiness and repentance. I hear the prophets crying out, "She was plucked up in fury, she was cast down to the ground, and the east wind dried up her fruit: her strong rods were broken and withered; the fire consumed them" (Ezekiel 19:12).

It is a day of vengeance and judgment against sin. The Lord has promised to judge His people who "hath done despite to the grace of God." "For we know him that hath said, Vengeance belongeth unto me, I will recompense, saith the Lord. And again, The Lord shall judge his people. It is a fearful thing to fall into the hands of the living God" (Hebrews 10:30,31).

Sudden Destruction Prophesied

We have been clearly warned of sudden destruction falling upon us. The prophets have all warned of a consuming fire of judgment upon a last-day people who boasted she sat as a queen in prosperity and was beyond the possibility of destruction. Isaiah warned, "For he bringeth down them that dwell on high; the lofty city, he layeth it low; he layeth it low, even to the ground; he bringeth it even to the dust" (Isaiah 26:5).

Joshua prophesied of a people who in the latter times would quickly perish from off the land. "When ye have transgressed the covenant of the Lord your God, which he commanded you, and have gone and served other gods, and bowed yourselves to them; then shall the anger of the Lord be kindled against you, and ye shall perish quickly from off the good land which he hath given unto you" (Joshua 23:16). This is a principle of judgment throughout God's Word.

The prophet Zephaniah sounded a trumpet about a

coming day of darkness, gloom, and devouring fire. His dual prophecy spoke of "a speedy riddance" of the whole land. "Neither their silver nor their gold shall be able to deliver them in the day of the Lord's wrath; but the whole land shall be devoured by the fire of his jealousy: for he shall make even a speedy riddance of all them that dwell in the land" (Zephaniah 1:18). Every prophet seems pressed by the suddenness and quickness of God's devouring, melting fire falling on those who are under divine judgment.

John saw in a vision the destruction of one-third of the earth's population by fire and brimstone. The enemy would have an exceeding great army and armaments which would spew "out of their 'mouths' fire, smoke, and brimstone" (Revelation 9:16,17)—which I take to mean nuclear missiles.

As a result of this fiery "issue," one-third of mankind is destroyed. "By these three was the third part of men killed, by the fire, and by the smoke, and by the brimstone, which issued out of their mouths" (Revelation 9:18).

Woe to you who are at ease in Zion. He warned you that all lukewarm believers would be spewed out of His mouth. You spoke the word of faith, creating for yourselves riches, increase of goods, and you spent your faith in providing for all your selfish needs. Now you can say you have need of nothing. You are "clothed in fine linen, and purple, and scarlet, and decked with gold, and precious stones, and pearls" (Revelation 18:16).

In one hour it will all be gone! The stock market will burn—with all the buildings, the investments. The skyscrapers will melt; the fire of divine vengeance will turn cities into polluted wildernesses. Our government, our transportation systems, our food supplies, our communications networks (radio, television)—all will be lost in **one hour**! Read it—it's all there! "And it shall be, as with the people, so with the priest; as with the servant, so with his master; as with the maid, so with her mistress; as with the buyer, so with the seller; as with the lender, so with the borrower; as with the taker of usury, so with the giver of usury to him. The land shall be utterly emptied, and utterly spoiled: for the Lord hath spoken this word. The city of confusion is broken down: every house is shut up, that no man may come in. When thus it shall be in the midst of the land among the people, there shall be as a shaking of an olive tree, and as the gleaning grapes when the vintage is done" (Isaiah 24:2,3,10,13). Isaiah is clearly speaking about these latter days.

I believe Moses saw our day and prophesied by the Spirit that God would devour in the latter days with burning heat. His prophecy is a chilling reminder of what is coming. He said, "For a fire is kindled in mine anger, and shall burn unto the lowest hell, and shall consume the earth with her increase, and set on fire the foundations of the mountains. I will heap mischiefs upon them; I will spend mine arrows upon them. They shall be burnt with hunger, and devoured with burning heat, and with bitter destruction: I will also send the teeth of beasts upon them, with the poison of serpents of the dust" (Deuteronomy 32:22-24). Could the arrows he saw be missiles? Is it the Russian beast that sinks her teeth into "a nation void of counsel" (Deuteronomy 32:28)? Hear his plea, "O that they were wise, that they understood this, that they would consider their latter end!" (Deuteronomy 32:29). The entire vision describes what will befall in the latter days. These are those latter days, and we are the seed of Israel.

How could we have missed the prophet Joel's warnings all these years? He clearly predicted blood, fire, and pillars of smoke on the earth, ascending into the heavens—**before** the great and the terrible day of the Lord. "And I will shew wonders in the heavens and in the earth, blood, and fire, and pillars of smoke. The sun shall be turned into darkness, and the moon into blood, before the great and the terrible day of the Lord come" (Joel 2:30,31).

What a wonder in the heavens, as from the earth huge mushroom-type pillars of smoke rise. And also, how true that on that blood, fire, and smoke day, all in this land who have called on Christ's name in fullness will be glorified. "And it shall come to pass, that whosoever shall call on the name of the Lord shall be delivered: for in mount Zion and in Jerusalem shall be deliverance, as the Lord hath said, and in the remnant whom the Lord shall call" (Joel 2:32).

Paul spoke of a day of fiery vengeance coming on those who flaunt sin. "For if we sin wilfully after that we have received the knowledge of the truth, there remaineth no more sacrifice for sins, but a certain fearful looking for of judgment and fiery indignation, which shall devour the adversaries" (Hebrews 10:26,27).

Think of the "lady in the harbor"—the Statue of Liberty. Isaiah warned of sudden destruction upon a proud lady. "And thou saidst, I shall be a lady for ever: so that thou didst not lay these things to thy heart, neither didst remember the latter end of it. Therefore hear now this, thou that art given to pleasures, that dwellest carelessly, that sayest in thine heart, I am, and none else beside me; I shall not sit as a widow, neither shall I know the loss of children: but these two things shall come to thee in a moment in one day, the loss of children, and widowhood: they shall come upon thee in their perfection for the multitude of thy sorceries, and for the great abundance of thine enchantments. For thou hast trusted in thy wickedness: thou hast said, None seeth me. Thy wisdom and thy knowledge, it hath perverted thee; and thou hast said in thine heart, I am, and none else beside me. Therefore shall evil come upon thee; thou shalt not know from whence it riseth: and mischief shall fall upon thee; thou shalt not be able to put it off: and desolation shall come upon thee suddenly, which thou shalt not know" (Isaiah 47:7-11).

Isaiah said, "A curse has devoured the earth, and they that dwell therein are desolate: therefore the inhabitants of the earth are burned, and few men left" (Isaiah 24:6). Not a flood this time, but a devouring fire. "And the people shall be as the burnings of lime: as thorns cut up shall they be burned in the fire. The sinners in Zion are afraid: fearfulness hath surprised thy hypocrites. Who among us shall dwell with the devouring fire? Who among us shall dwell with everlasting burnings?" (Isaiah 33:12,14).

Isaiah saw the Lord coming in a chariot of fire to execute judgment, and many will be slain. "For, behold, the Lord will come with fire, and with his chariots like a whirlwind, to render his anger with fury, and his rebuke with flames of fire. For by fire and by his sword will the Lord plead with all flesh: and the slain of the Lord shall be many" (Isaiah 66:15,16).

What a horrific description of a hydrogen holocaust Isaiah gives. "The foundations of the earth do shake. The earth is utterly broken down, the earth is clean dissolved, the earth is moved exceedingly. The earth shall reel to and fro like a drunkard, and shall be removed like a cottage; and the transgression thereof shall be heavy upon it; and it shall fall, and not rise again. Then the moon shall be confounded, and the sun ashamed..." (Isaiah 24:18-20,23).

A Sudden Dissolving—A Meltdown

Make no mistake about it, God's Word clearly warns a great dissolving will happen. I believe it is imminent. It is not incidental that Paul spoke of the "dissolving" of the physical body. "For we know that if our earthly house of this tabernacle were dissolved, we have a building of God, an house not made with hands, eternal in the heavens" (2 Corinthians 5:1). Peter warned, "Seeing then that all these things shall be dissolved, what manner of persons ought ye to be in all holy conversation and godliness, looking for and earnestly desiring the coming of the day of God, wherein the heavens being on fire shall be dissolved, and the elements shall melt with intense heat" (2 Peter 3:11,12). David prophesied, "The earth and all the inhabitants thereof are dissolved: I bear up the pillars of it. For in the hand of the Lord there is a cup, and the wine is red; it is full of mixture; and he poureth out of the same: but the dregs thereof, all the wicked of the earth shall wring them out, and drink them" (Psalm 75:3,8).

God will "melt" America, just as He promised to do to Israel. "As they gather silver, and brass, and iron, and lead, and tin, into the midst of the furnace, to blow the fire upon it, to melt it; so will I gather you in mine anger and in my fury, and I will leave you there, and melt you. Yea, I will gather you, and blow upon you in the fire of my wrath, and ye shall be melted in the midst thereof. As silver is melted in the midst of the furnace, so shall ye be melted in the midst thereof; and ye shall know that I the Lord have poured out my fury upon you" (Ezekiel 22:20-22).

America's cup of iniquity is full; the bear has prepared and is set to act—it is now only a matter of time. From over the North Pole the deadly missiles will come. Fear and some kind of supernatural impulse will cause the enemy to make the first strike. "For the spoilers shall come unto her from the north, saith the Lord" (Jeremiah 51:48). They themselves will be terrorized by the destruction and havoc they unleashed upon the earth. "The Lord of hosts hath purposed it, to stain the pride of all glory, and to bring into contempt all the honourable of the earth. He stretched out his hand over the sea, he shook the kingdoms: the Lord hath given a commandment against the merchant city, to destroy the strong hold thereof" (Isaiah 23:9,11).

Zechariah spoke of a day when God would "gather all nations against Jerusalem to battle...and the Lord shall fight against those nations" (Zechariah 14:2,3). America will never fight against Israel, nor will we protect her. God will protect Israel and send fire on us! If you cannot believe that fiery judgment is near, you must believe it is inevitable. Zephaniah proved it: "Therefore wait ye upon me, saith the Lord, until the day that I rise up to the prey: for my determination is to gather the nations, that I may assemble the kingdoms, to pour upon them mine indignation, even all my fierce anger: for all the earth shall be devoured with the fire of my jealousy" (Zephaniah 3:8).

The prophet Isaiah puts it all beyond argument. If you believe God's Word is truth, then you must believe He is going to utterly empty and spoil any land that God judges. He wrote, "The land shall be utterly emptied, and utterly spoiled; for the Lord hath spoken this word" (Isaiah 24:3).

Our Great Armaments Will Be Worthless

"Behold, I will bring...all evil that I have pronounced...because they hardened their necks, that they might not hear my words" (Jeremiah 19:15).

Jeremiah gathered all the elders of Israel and took them into the valley of the son of Hinnom. There he broke an earthen pot into many pieces and prophesied to them these words, "Thus saith the Lord...I will bring evil upon this place, such as all who hear, their ears shall tingle" (Jeremiah 19:3).

The prophet told them incredible things, things that seemed so unlikely. It was a time of great peace and prosperity; yet, an approaching day of slaughter, of horrible plagues, and a day that God was going to shiver to pieces their nation, their cities, just like the vessel he smashed into many pieces (Jeremiah 19:6-11 Spurrell[1]). They were warned God would make useless their weapons of war, that all their armaments could not save them from God's wrath (Jeremiah 21:4). God said to them, "I myself will fight against you!" (Jeremiah 21:5).

That is an outright warning to America. Our huge stockpiles of weapons are but so many sticks and stones—useless against what God has planned against us. What was said of ancient Babylon will be said of modern Babylon, "The mighty men of Babylon have forborn to fight, they have remained in their holds: their might hath failed; they became as women: they have burned her dwellingplaces; her bars are broken" (Jeremiah 51:30). This is why there will be no retaliatory strikes from this nation or its allies; because of the suddenness and finality of it all, we will "forebare to fight," and our missiles will remain in their hold. Our might will fail us in the hour of judgment. Our allies will "become as women" and surrender immediately.

God is going to shake all that can be shaken. He is going to shiver into pieces all we once held sacred and dear to us. He is going to judge this nation with such severity, it will cause the ears of all nations to tingle. The nations of the world will hiss at us with astonishment. "And I will make this city [land] desolate, and an hissing; every one that passeth thereby shall be astonished and hiss because of all the plagues thereof"

---

[1] Helen Spurrell, 1892. Original Hebrew edition of the Holy Bible. Out of print.

(Jeremiah 19:8). God Himself will fight against this nation, and whereas He once desired for us only good, now He will plan for us only evil because of the hardness of our hearts. "Though Babylon should mount up to heaven, and though she should fortify the height of her strength, yet from me shall spoilers come unto her, saith the Lord" (Jeremiah 51:53).

Our wound, like Israel's, is incurable now. "For thus saith the Lord, Thy bruise is incurable, and thy wound is serious....thou hast no healing medicines" (Jeremiah 30:12,13). No astrologer, no prognosticator can stop the judgment coming. They may mock and sneer; but they, too, will burn. "Thou art wearied in the multitude of thy counsels. Let now the astrologers, the stargazers, the monthly prognosticators, stand up, and save thee from these things that shall come upon thee. Behold, they shall be as stubble; the fire shall burn them; they shall not deliver themselves from the power of the flame: there shall not be a coal to warm at, nor fire to sit before it" (Isaiah 47:13,14).

God Will Judge Russia With Supernatural Fire

God Himself will deal with Russia with supernatural destruction beyond all description. A frantic search for peace will fail. "Destruction cometh; and they shall seek peace, and there shall be none" (Ezekiel 7:25). The enemy will cry peace, and it will appear that peace is possible while all the while they are preparing for war. America will suffer the first strokes of vengeance. At a later time, when Russia invades the Holy Land, God will Himself destroy all but a sixth of that nation. "And I will turn thee back, and leave but the sixth part of thee, and will cause thee to come up from the north parts, and will bring thee upon the mountains of Israel. Thou shalt fall upon the mountains of Israel,

14

thou, and all thy bands, and the people that is with thee: I will give thee unto the ravenous birds of every sort, and to the beasts of the field to be devoured" (Ezekiel 39:2,4).

Russia invades Israel because the American eagle is no longer there to defend her. The defense of Israel will not be our battle but the Lord's—so that Israel will give all glory to God. "And I will plead against him with pestilence and with blood; and I will rain upon him, and upon his bands, and upon the many people that are with him, an overflowing rain, and great hailstones, fire, and brimstone. Thus will I magnify myself, and sanctify myself; and I will be known in the eyes of many nations, and they shall know that I am the Lord" (Ezekiel 38:22,23).

Warning Signs

Before the great holocaust there will be smaller holocausts—the oil fields of the middle east will be ablaze, and the smoke will rise night and day as a warning of the greater holocaust yet to come. There will be bombs falling on oil fields, on shipping docks and storage tanks. There will be panic among all oil producers, and shippers, and upon all nations dependent on that oil.

Soon, very soon, an economic nightmare will explode into reality. What frightful news it will be! "O thou that dwellest upon many waters, abundant in treasures, thine end is come, and the measure of thy covetousness" (Jeremiah 51:13). America is about to face a time of mass hysteria, as banks close and financial institutions crumble and our economy spins totally out of control. Gold and silver will also lose their value. "They shall cast their silver in the streets, and their gold shall be removed: their silver and their gold shall not be able to deliver them in a day of the wrath of the Lord: they shall not satisfy their souls, neither fill their bowels: because it is the stumblingblock of their iniquity" (Ezekiel 7:19). The chaos that is coming cannot be stopped by our government. Ezekiel warned, "The hands of the people of the land shall be troubled: I will do unto them after their way, and according to their deserts will I judge them" (Ezekiel 7:27). These prophecies once again reveal God's judgmental decrees to wicked nations.

Scoff if you choose, but the underlying fears about a collapse will soon become a tragic reality. Numerous cracks will appear in our fragile prosperity, and soon even the most pessimistic will know in their hearts that a total collapse is certain. Senators and congressmen will sit in stunned silence as they realize no one can stop the tailspin into chaos. Business, political, and economic leaders will be terrorized by its suddenness and its far-reaching effect. "Son of man, when the land sinneth against me by trespassing grievously, then will I stretch out mine hand upon it, and will break the staff of the bread thereof, and will send famine upon it, and will cut off man and beast from it" (Ezekiel 14:13). The great holocaust follows an economic collapse in America. The enemy will make its move when we are weak and helpless.

God Goes With His People Through the Fire

God did not keep the three Hebrew children from the fire—He delivered them in it. Christ went with them through the fire, and, whereas they came back to ruin, we will be translated to glory. A fiery holocaust to those who walk in white is not a terror! To them, it is instant resurrection and not the wrath of God. What is a holocaust to an overcomer who can honestly say, "Live or die, I am the Lord's!" "Wherefore glorify ye the Lord in the fires, even the name of the Lord God of Israel in the isles of the sea" (Isaiah 24:15).

It is impossible for an overcomer to be touched by God's wrath, and the coming holocaust will not be tribulation, but glory to the saints. God's wrath is reserved for the unbeliever and the ungodly. However, it has been God's way from the beginning to deliver His people in, during, and out of judgment and wrath. "Behold, I have refined thee, but not with silver; I have chosen thee in the furnace of affliction" (Isaiah 48:10). The flood was a holocaust also, and Noah and his family went through it.

David said the judgment on the wicked is at the same time salvation for the meek. "Thou didst cause judgment to be heard from heaven; the earth feared, and was still, when God arose to judgment, to save all the meek of the earth" (Psalm 76:8,9). The judgment that damns the lost saves the meek and holy! I care less about surviving here on earth; I and all my overcoming brothers and sisters are already in the ark—Christ Jesus the Lord. We have something much better planned for us; we get to be glorified! "And the Lord their God shall save them in that day as the flock of his people: for they shall be as the stones of a crown, lifted up as an ensign upon his land" (Zechariah 9:16).

Are we so blind, so earthbound, that we want God to keep us alive physically, only to live in a contaminated, hostile environment? Why can't we see that a holocaust can only dissolve this earthly body; but that very dissolving brings us into a celestial one. It will be instant glory. How can we who are already dead to the world be adversely affected by a holocaust? As for me, I died to the world—its pleasures, its pains, its destruction—so that a meltdown simply brings me into the fullness of an inheritance I already possess in measure. I am already enjoying the power of an endless life. "Who is made, not after the law of a carnal commandment, but after the power of an endless life" (Hebrews 7:16).

God is going to actually hold our hand through this great consuming fire. He promised, "For I the Lord thy God will hold thy right hand, saying unto thee, Fear not; I will help thee" (Isaiah 41:13). Overcomers will not even be hurt by the flames as others. That is clearly promised in God's Word. "When thou walkest through the fire, thou shalt not be burned; neither shall the flame kindle upon thee" (Isaiah 43:2).

Are Christians going to suffer when God shakes this nation with earthquakes and economic disasters? Yes! There will be much suffering and hardship, but God will meet the necessities of His overcomers. He will comfort their hearts, and as they see these frightful things coming upon the nation and the world, they will be at peace, saying, "God warned us! We are prepared! We knew it all along, and we are not afraid. Our blessed Savior will go with us through it all."

To me, going home to Jesus in a sudden fiery holocaust is an escape from God's wrath. How can it be wrath when He takes me by the hand and leads me to paradise? God's chosen can look at every disaster right in its fury and declare, "Nothing can move me; I am safe in the palm of His hand."

America Will Not Repent

Jeremiah delivered a dual prophecy out of a potter's house. It was directed to ancient Israel, but also to Israel the church. His message is again being sounded by the Holy Spirit and will soon be fulfilled in our day. "O house of Israel, cannot I do with you as this potter? saith the Lord. Behold, as the clay is in the potter's hand, so are ye in mine hand, O house of Israel. At what instant I shall speak concerning a nation, and concerning a kingdom, to pluck up, and to pull down, and to destroy it" (Jeremiah 18:6,7).

God claims the right to pluck up, pull down, and destroy at an instant a nation, a congregation, a minister or ministry that becomes marred and useless to Him. God made this nation a beautiful vessel in His hand over two hundred years ago. He set it in a good land and blessed its founding fathers. But evil has become so great, disobedience so widespread, God has declared, "I will pluck it up, pull it down, destroy it, as it seemeth good to me." "And at what instant I shall speak concerning a nation, and concerning a kingdom, to build and to plant it. If it do evil in my sight, that it obey not my voice, then I will repent of the good, wherewith I said I would benefit them" (Jeremiah 18:9,10).

This nation has not repented but, rather, has turned its back on the Word of the Lord, and now God will do what He said He would do. Only a remnant now follows the Lord with all their hearts, living in holy surrender and full communion with Him. There has been no deep heart repentance. We have leaders who are thought of as "Christians" who publicly confess they don't even know what it means to be born again. Only lip service is given to God, and the popular evangelical Christianity of this hour is nothing but political and lukewarm, at its best. This nation, its government, its churches, gives the Lord Jesus mere acknowledgement but not heart repentance. We have great moral indignation against poverty, abortion, crime, injustice, and that is commendable—but we have not enthroned Jesus Christ as Lord and King in our hearts. Millions claim to be Christians, yet only a very small number are entering the straight gate. If God favors America with more time and prosperity, it will only increase the wickedness and rebellion, making judgment even more certain. "Let favour be shewed to the wicked, yet will he not learn righteousness: in the land of uprightness will he deal unjustly, and will not behold the majesty of the Lord. Lord, when thy hand is lifted up, they will not see: but they shall see, and be ashamed for their envy at the people; yea, the fire of thine enemies shall devour them" (Isaiah 26:10,11).

God promised to preserve America only it if turned from its evil. At the very moment of true repentance and turning from evil, He promised to change His mind and hold back judgment. Yet, nothing is clearer in all the Word of God than His threat against a corrupt nation, to "scatter that nation as with an east wind before the enemy; and I will shew them my back, and not my face, in the day of their downfall" (Jeremiah 18:17).

I see almighty God even now slowly turning His back on this nation! America is on the verge of committing the unpardonable sin by resisting the Holy Ghost. Soon, there will be repentance only for individuals, but not the nation. What more could He have done for America? Could He have been any more patient than He has been? "What could have been done more to my vineyard, that I have not done in it? Wherefore, when I looked that it should bring forth grapes, brought it forth wild grapes?" (Isaiah 5:4). "I have spread out my hands all the day unto a rebellious people, which walketh in a way that was not good, after their own thoughts" (Isaiah 65:2).

The unthinkable is going to happen to America and parts of Canada, and few will believe it. The prophets of peace and prosperity will reply, "God has promised to keep us from the day of wrath, because we have kept the word of His patience" (Revelation 3:10). This nation has **not** kept God's word, nor has the church. Like in the church of Sardis, there are only a few who have not defiled their garments and who walk with Christ in robes of white. It is said, "No plague shall come nigh thy dwelling" (Psalm 91:10). But disobedience and rebellion abort the promises of safety and protection. [See Hebrews 10:26,27]

Don't listen to the prophets of peace and prosperity. They are deceived. They have not heard the true Word of God. They are not of the spirit of Elijah, Isaiah, Ezekiel, and Jeremiah. They have not been weeping and travailing over the sins of the nation and God's people. God truly has devised a plan, a frightful series of calamities against this nation; and His final appeal is going forth, a final call to return and forsake all evil doings. "Thus shall Babylon sink, and shall not rise from the evil that I will bring upon her" (Jeremiah 51:64).

Ezekiel was lifted by the Holy Spirit and taken to the Lord's house where he saw twenty-five spiritual leaders, princes, who sat about mocking the warnings of impending doom and making plans to build and prosper. The Lord said to Ezekiel, "Son of man, these are the men that plan mischief, and give wicked counsel to this people. They say, Judgment is not near; let us build houses" (Ezekiel 11:1-3).

The warnings of Ezekiel and the hardness of the people's hearts produced a boastful cynicism. Listen to their fatalistic attitude, "This city is the caldron, and we be the flesh" (Ezekiel 11:3). In other words, "If fire is coming, we choose to live it up to the end and stew in our own juices!" This is the attitude of the gay community now; it is the attitude of the rich, lukewarm church; it is the attitude of millions of Americans who have heard dire warnings for so long they no longer are moved by them. We have had "hurricane" parties where drunken Americans refused to evacuate Gulf Coast islands, but preferred to party in the storm. Many died, mocking the fury of the hurricane and God Himself!

What we see in America today is one great holocaust party, with millions drunk, high, shaking their fists at

God, daring Him to send the bombs. They bellow out their curses, saying, "The Lord hath forsaken the earth, and the Lord seeth not" (Ezekiel 9:9).

America Parties on the Brink Of Judgment

Thousands of Christians have already seen the handwriting on the wall. What do sin-bound people do just prior to judgment? Like Belshazzar, they party while the enemy gathers at the gate. A Christian rock group yelled into the microphone, "Come, let's party for Jesus." And it is party time for multitudes of God's people. With the sword of judgment hanging overhead, they say by their actions, "It is hopeless anyhow. We will have a fling! We will not resist our lusts anymore. We will do as we please."

Adultery, fornication, divorce, remarriage—this is God's people doing as they please. This is the last-day Israel following in the steps of Judah and Jerusalem. God can hardly believe it. He said, "Ask ye now among the heathen, who hath heard such things: the virgin of Israel hath done a very horrible thing" (Jeremiah 18:13).

God's people are doing a very horrible thing that not even the heathen would do. They don't forsake their gods; but "my people hath forgotten me, they have worshipped vanity, and they have caused them to stumble in their ways from the ancient paths, in a way not exalted" (Jeremiah 18:15 Spurrell).

How horrible, saith the Lord. The people of God stumbling blindly, forsaking the old paths of holiness, setting their hearts on success, prosperity, and all kinds of other vanities. Is it not true, the Christian path for most today is **not the exalted way**?

No wonder God is now showing us His back and not His face! We are forgetting Him! Hear it and weep, O church of God—"My people have forgotten me days without number" (Jeremiah 2:32). Only a church that has forgotten God, only a church bound by lust could become so immoral and lax. Only a hopeless people could give themselves over to such wickedness. These are those who, being reproved, hardened their hearts. And a hard and hopeless heart loses all fear of God, death, or judgment.

Who Will Listen?

We don't like to hear these words. They are too hard, too incredible, too much to comprehend. How can this nation, now so proud, powerful, and prosperous, suddenly fall and become a place of slaughter and plagues? Who wants to believe it? Who is close enough to God to hear the sounding of His trumpet? Certainly not the false prophets like Pashur, the chief leader in the house of the Lord. He slapped Jeremiah's face and threw him in jail for prophesying such gloom and doom. The religious leaders, priests, and prophets were all telling the people that good days were ahead, a time of national glory, success, peace, and endless prosperity. And they borrowed their soothing messages from one another, encouraging thousands with their lies. They went about prophesying their nation and people would not suffer destruction. "Because ye have said, We have made a covenant with death, and with hell are we at agreement; when the overflowing scourge shall pass through, it shall not come unto us; for we have made lies our refuge, and under falsehood have we hid ourselves. And your covenant with death shall be disannulled, and your agreement with hell shall not stand; when the overflowing scourge shall pass through, then ye shall be trodden down by it" (Isaiah 28:15,18). Jeremiah thundered at them, "Thou shalt die,...and all thy friends, to whom thou hast prophesied lies" (Jeremiah 20:6).

God's word of judgment has never been heard or accepted by the church or its leaders. Elijah stood alone for God before 400 prophets of Baal. Jeremiah stood alone before the entire religious systems of Judah and Israel. The greatest enemies to his message were the leaders in God's house.

Why does God make trumpet calls and warn of impending judgment? First, to awaken His true bride; and second, to justify His wrath upon the lukewarm and the sinners who reject. It has been prophesied that at midnight a cry will be made and the wise virgins will hear and prepare. Paul warned, "And that, knowing the time, that now it is high time to awake out of sleep: for now is our salvation nearer than when we believed. The night is far spent, the day is at hand: let us therefore cast off the works of darkness, and let us put on the armour of light" (Romans 13:11,12).

God Is Separating His Remnant

I see something happening in America that I have not seen in my lifetime. There is a supernatural, quiet purging and separation going on.

The covetous Christians are flocking to hear their pillow prophets predicting endless prosperity and peace; and they sweetly prophesy nothing but good things to come. Jeremiah said, "They have belied the Lord, and said, It is not he; neither shall evil come upon us; neither shall we see sword nor famine: And the prophets shall become wind, and the word is not in them: thus shall it be done unto them" (Jeremiah 5:12,13). These are those who are buying, selling, eating, and drinking, as if judgment was a figment of the imagination. They are lounging on beds of ease; they sense no danger; they are fast asleep and slumbering on the brink of a holocaust. They wink at sin and refuse to renounce wickedness in the Lord's house. They are blinded and deceived and don't know it! They reject the warning of Isaiah, "Now therefore be ye not mockers, lest your bands be made strong: for I have heard from the Lord God of hosts a consumption, even determined upon the whole earth" (Isaiah 28:22).

But the overcomers are coming out into a place of holiness, intercessory prayer, and separation from all that is of this world. They have turned to the Lord with all their hearts, having renounced all hidden works of darkness; they are being purged and purified; they are hearing the sounds of the gathering storm; and they have been warned to get their houses in order, for their Redeemer is coming to Zion! They have made Christ their hiding place. "And a man shall be as an hiding place from the wind, and a covert from the tempest; as rivers of water in a dry place, as the shadow of a great rock in a weary land" (Isaiah 32:2). For a small moment He must leave us to the melting elements, but soon after, will gather us to Himself. "For a small moment have I forsaken thee; but with great mercies will I gather thee. In a little wrath I hid my face from thee for a moment; but with everlasting kindness will I have mercy on thee, saith the Lord thy Redeemer. For the mountains shall depart, and the hills be removed; but my kindness shall not depart from thee; neither shall the covenant of my peace be removed, saith the Lord that hath mercy on thee" (Isaiah 54:7,8,10).

The bride of Christ is preparing herself! The true body of Christ on earth is coming together in the Spirit, and we are beginning to recognize the bridehood by the fruits of righteousness. The bride of Christ will stand before the impending holocaust with great peace. "Thou wilt keep him in perfect peace, whose mind is stayed on thee: because he trusteth in thee" (Isaiah 26:3).

God is saying, "Come, my people, enter thou into thy

chambers, and shut thy doors about thee: hide thyself as it were for a little moment, until the indignation be overpast. For, behold, the Lord cometh out of his place to punish the inhabitants of the earth for their iniquity: the earth also shall disclose her blood, and shall no more cover her slain" (Isaiah 26:20,21). This does not mean we quit evangelizing. Never! It means we do it with our souls hidden in Him, protected by a wall of fire.

Let the pillow prophets smile condescendingly at our holy rage and our urgent cries of judgment. Not one of them can hinder God's plan to chastise this godless nation. The time is soon coming that not even the prayers of a Moses or a Samuel can change God's mind. "Your iniquities have separated between you and your God, and your sins have hid his face from you, that he will not hear" (Isaiah 59:2). God said, "Though Moses and Samuel stood before me, yet my mind could not be toward this people: cast them out of my sight, and let them go forth. Thou hast forsaken me, saith the Lord, thou art gone backward: therefore will I stretch out my hand against thee, and destroy thee; I am weary with repenting. And I will fan them with a fan in the gates of the land; I will bereave them of children, I will destroy my people, since they return not from their ways....for a fire is kindled in mine anger, which shall burn upon you" (Jeremiah 15:1,6,7,14).

Even with such dire predictions of what was about to happen, Jeremiah offered them a last chance. "Therefore thus saith the Lord, If thou return, then will I bring thee again, and thou shalt stand before me: and if thou take forth the precious from the vile, thou shalt be as my mouth....I will be with thee to save and deliver thee, and I will deliver you out of the hand of the wicked" (Jeremiah 15:19-21).

This trumpet call is not the wild rantings of a few

fanatics and date-setting doom-sayers. This same prophecy has been heard and is being preached by growing numbers of devout, praying, interceeding men and women of God. God's Word declares, "Surely the Lord God will do nothing, but he revealeth his secret unto his servants the prophets" (Amos 3:7). Also, "The Lord God hath spoken, who can but prophesy?" (Amos 3:8).

Shall We Hide or Evangelize?

God does not need America to evangelize the world. We have failed in this mission. Our nation still spends more money each year for dog food than for missions. There will be one last great ingathering, and it is even now happening. The gospel will be published to all the world by a great army of witnesses indigenous to every nation on earth. It is the Lord's last harvest. Even now the Spirit of God is raising up a thriving body of witnesses in China. South America and Africa will be covered with powerful witnesses from their own lands. Mexico and South America are open to the gospel and young evangelists are being raised up. They will not need missions boards, ordinations, large amounts of money, and fancy equipment. They will live on pennies, as the early disciples did; and in a short time they will cover the earth with the gospel. And they will point to God's fiery judgment on this careless, rich, modern Babylon as a sign the end is near. Even then, the wicked will not repent, according to John's revelation.

The rest of the world will see this awesome nuclear holocaust and remain unrepentant. Two-thirds of the earth will go on seeking prosperity, worshipping Satan, and mocking God. The discipline on America will not humble the rest of the wicked. "And the rest of the men which were not killed by these plagues yet repented not of the works of their hands, that they should not worship devils, and idols of gold, and silver, and brass, and stone, and of wood: which neither can see, nor hear, nor walk: neither repented they of their murders, nor of their sorceries, nor of their fornication, nor of their thefts" (Revelation 9:20,21).

What America could not do with all of its millions, all of its electronic gimmicks, all of its expensive media methods, the Holy Spirit will accomplish in a short time with a Gideon's army of poor and simple evangelists from Third World countries; and the rest of the world will hear the gospel. A remnant of overcomers from all nations will be raised up in righteousness. In spite of full gospel light shining forth, the majority will turn to Satan and be given over to lust. The Bible does not say that judgment on America awaits world evangelism. It is only His return that awaits the fruit of the harvest. I see it so clearly!

Seeing therefore that the time is short, let us be diligent. Knowing the hour is late, let us redeem the time. We will work while it is yet day, before the night comes and no man can work. We will preach and teach and go into all nations witnessing—as though judgment will never come. We will believe for the greatest outpouring of the Spirit ever. We will pray for one last great harvest. The overcomers who are ready for anything are the most effective witnesses. This is the time to give ourselves to missions, to bringing in the last harvest.

No hiding! No mountain cabins of escape! No caves or shelters! No stockpiles of food or weapons or water. God's holy remnant can look death right in the face and say, "I fear you not. There is no more sting, no more terror. I am ready to be offered."

The bride of Christ is already feeling the magnetic pull to the marriage supper of the Lamb. Like Paul, the bridehood will have a great longing to go to be with Him; but for the sake of lost souls, unconverted families, they rejoice and labor here without fear or anxiety.

I intend to stay on the streets, preaching to junkies and harlots. I intend to write and distribute literature worldwide. I will be fully occupied in His service when the end comes. So don't try to put aside this trumpet call as escapism or a damper on world evangelism. That would be an outright lying accusation. Now that I know judgment is at the door, I work with an even greater urgency.

The greatest Holy Ghost outpouring in the history of mankind is already happening—but only the overcoming remnant are responding. The evil and lukewarm wax worse and worse, as prophesied; but the righteous are receiving oil in full measure for their vessels and their lamps. Soon, we will go out to meet Him—suddenly, we will be with Him! **Glory!**

In the next chapter, I want to show you what the prophets called "that horrible thing in God's house"— shepherds, pastors, and the people of God given to adultery, fornication, and sensuality.

Chapter 2

The "Horrible Thing" in God's House: Adultery, Fornication, Divorce

"I have seen also in the prophets of Jerusalem an horrible thing: they commit adultery, and walk in lies: they strengthen also the hands of evildoers, that none doth return from his wickedness: they are all of them unto me as Sodom, and the inhabitants thereof as Gomorrah" (Jeremiah 23:14).

Just before God judges this nation He is going to purge and judge His house, its worshippers, and its ministers. This trumpet call has nothing to do with the wicked masses outside God's house. Judgment is beginning in the house of the Lord and He has said, "Woe unto them that seek deep to hide their counsel from the Lord, and their works are in the dark, and they say, Who seeth us? and who knoweth us?" (Isaiah 29:15).

I bring to the body of Christ and all true ministers of the sanctuary a message from God's throne. It is an ultimatum and a warning to all who are ready to hear the truth. The message of this chapter will save a host of adulterers from being given over to their sin, and it will condemn many others in their iniquity and could be for them their final warning. Those who refuse to repent and turn from their adulterous, fornicating ways could be released to their sins, harden their hearts, and be forever lost. It is that serious and momentous in the eyes of God. Only the pure in heart shall see God.

I know it; God knows it; and so does every other sanctified, praying saint: the church and the ministry is rife with adultery, fornication, eroticism, and divorce. "They were as fed horses in the morning: every one neighed after his neighbor's wife. Shall I not visit for these things? saith the Lord: and shall not my soul be avenged on such a nation as this?" (Jeremiah 5:8,9). Literally millions of Christians and multitudes of ministers are trapped in a satanic snare of lust. They are drunk, not with wine but with lust. They are fast asleep in their sins; a deep slumber from the Lord has been put upon them because of their refusal to turn from their wickedness. Lusting, sin-corrupted prophets and leaders broke Isaiah's heart and angered him. He cried out, "Stay yourselves, and wonder; cry ye out, and cry: they are drunken, but not with wine; they stagger, but not with strong drink. For the Lord hath poured out upon you the spirit of deep sleep, and hath closed your eyes: the prophets and your rulers, the seers hath he covered" (Isaiah 29:9,10).

Jeremiah's prophetic eye scanned the ministry of his day and of the last days, and what he saw made him weep and tremble. "Mine heart within me is broken because of the prophets; all my bones shake; I am like a drunken man, and like a man whom wine hath overcome, because of the Lord, and because of the words of his holiness. For the land is full of adulterers; for because of swearing the land mourneth; the pleasant places of the wilderness are dried up, and their course is evil, and their force is not right" (Jeremiah 23:9,10).

The prophet Hosea warned, "Ye have plowed wickedness, ye have reaped iniquity; ye have eaten the fruit of lies...therefore shall a tumult arise among thy people, and all thy fortresses shall be spoiled" (Hosea 10:13,14).

"Ye Have Corrupted the Covenant of Levi"

The Levites served the tabernacle of Moses, and they were a type of our present day ministry. Ministers and Christian workers are "the sons" of Levi. The covenant of Levi was their consecration as an everlasting offering unto the Lord. "And thou shalt set the Levites before Aaron, and before his sons, and offer them for an offering unto the Lord. Thus shalt thou separate the Levites from among the children of Israel: and the Levites shall be mine" (Numbers 8:13,14). "And thou shalt cleanse them" (Numbers 8:15).

The covenant included total separation, cleansing, and this: "They are wholly given unto me...I have taken them unto me" (Numbers 8:16). They were to live a life of holiness, purity, and be wholly given to the Lord. It included the "covenant of salt," an everlasting statute that only holy and consecrated things could be devoured by them (Numbers 18:19).

With that in mind, hear the blunt rebuke of the prophet Malachi as he delivered God's message to backslidden priests: "Ye are departed out of the way; ye have caused many to stumble at the law; ye have corrupted the covenant of Levi, saith the Lord of hosts" (Malachi 2:8). They had polluted themselves with that which was unclean.

Who were these ministers and priests who were no longer separated, no longer pure and holy, no longer wholly given to the Lord? They were those who were cheating on their wives, adulterers who were untrue— "The Lord hath been witness between thee and the wife of thy youth, against whom thou hast dealt treacherously: yet is she thy companion, and the wife of thy covenant" (Malachi 2:14).

These servants of the tabernacle could not give up their adulterous ways and their secret lovers, but they sure knew how to weep and confess. God wearied of their continued weeping and confessing because it produced no separation or laying down of their lust. "And this have ye done again, covering the altar of the Lord with tears, with weeping, and with crying out, insomuch that he regardeth not the offering any more, or receiveth it with good will at your hand" (Malachi 2:13).

These adulterous priests and ministers had "profaned the holiness of the Lord...and hath married the daughter of a strange god" (Malachi 2:11). That strange god was Eros, the god of sensuality and lust. I tell you, with God's holy fear trembling in my soul, that there are multitudes of pastors, evangelists, teachers, and Christian workers who are trampling the holiness of God and have made a covenant with lust. They are married to another in their hearts. They can say, "One has my name, the other has my heart. With one I'll remain, but to the other I'll be true." They have no intention of forsaking their treachery; they are addicted, they are committed to their secret sin, and many may already be beyond redemption. They rejected the Spirit's call to repentance and cleansing, and now they have been given over to their attraction. Jeremiah wept profusely when he saw the lies, treachery, and adultery among God's people. "Oh that I had in the wilderness a lodging place of wayfaring men; that I might leave my people, and go from them! for they be all adulterers, an assembly of treacherous men. And they bend their tongues like their bow for lies: but they are not valiant for the truth upon the earth; for they proceed from evil to evil, and they know not me, saith the Lord" (Jeremiah 9:2,3).

Oh, man of God—tremble at this curse God prepared for priests and ministers who refused to forsake their immorality. "The Lord will cut off the man that doeth this, the master and the scholar, out of the tabernacles of Jacob" (Malachi 2:12).

Not only will God cut off the anointing, unction, and blessings; He will humiliate the offender, destroy his credibility, and cast his ministry aside. God has reserved the most fearful prophecies for ministers who live and preach in sin. Man of God, if you still tremble at God's Word, if you hate your sin and want out, let this warning be your final ultimatum; and let it give you the courage and fear of God to finally run from your bondage. We dare not take lightly Malachi's prophecy to Israel. "If ye will not hear, and if ye will not lay it to heart, to give glory unto my name, saith the Lord of hosts, I will even send a curse upon you, and I will curse your blessings: yea, I have cursed them already, because ye do not lay it to heart. Behold, I will corrupt your seed, and spread dung upon your faces...and one shall take you away" (Malachi 2:2,3).

The servant of God, the layman, who is untrue to his wife, who cheats on her and finally abandons her to remarry another, is even now under God's anathema—especially if children are involved. God says of them, "you cursed children" (2 Peter 2:14). The seed, meaning the gospel they preach or write, is powerless. Death produces death. Outwardly, things may look good to the public eye, but God has a controversy with these adulterers, and the prophecy of failure will eventually be fulfilled. Only full and complete repentance and restoration can restore the blessings. But the minister who stands in the pulpit, while living in adultery, has iniquity in his lips; he is not walking as an example of holiness; and he is breaking the love commandments of the Lord; and he causes many to stumble. "But ye are departed out of the way; ye have caused many to stumble" (Malachi 2:8).

For that, God says, "Therefore have I also made you contemptible and base before all the people, according as ye have not kept my ways, but have been partial in the law" (Malachi 2:9).

Keep in mind this entire message and these warnings and threats are directed to "the messengers of the Lord of hosts" and to those priests who once walked in truth with peace and equity and who "had turned many people away from iniquity" (Malachi 2:6,7).

The tragic end of cheating, adulterous ministers is total blindness and loss of all discernment. They end up justifying their evil deeds and the iniquity in others. Their preaching becomes an abomination that "wearies" the Lord. "Yet we say, Wherein have we wearied him? When ye say, Every one that doeth evil is good in the sight of the Lord, and he delighteth in them; or, Where is the God of judgment?" (Malachi 2:17).

The preacher who scoffs at judgment, who refuses to publicly renounce sin, and who makes others comfortable in theirs is covering up his own secret sin. Somewhere in his life is a skeleton. Some hidden work of darkness has tainted his message, and he ends up preaching soothing things, good things, prosperous things. Their sins testify against them. "For our transgressions are multiplied before thee, and our sins testify against us: for our transgressions are with us; and as for our iniquities, we know them; in transgressing and lying against the Lord, and departing away from our God, speaking oppression and revolt, conceiving and uttering from the heart words of falsehood" (Isaiah 59:12,13).

Ezekiel's Amazing Vision Of Our Time

In the tenth chapter of Ezekiel there is a shattering vision of what God is about to do just prior to His chastising this nation. This vision has been confusing for centuries, but now the Holy Spirit is making its truth known through His praying servants. It refers directly to our day, and it confirms the fiery judgments soon to fall. Also, it speaks about the last dealings God will have with the church and the final exposure and judgment of all hidden sin.

El Shaddai is Jehovah revealed as "the roar of thunder" (Psalm 29). It was El Shaddai that Ezekiel saw appearing in the firmament over the earth, sitting on a sapphire throne and coming to roar in thunderous judgment upon sinful mankind. "Then I looked, and behold, in the firmament that was above the head of the cherubims there appeared over them as it were a sapphire stone, as the appearance of the likeness of a throne. And he spake unto the man clothed with linen, and said, Go in between the wheels, even under the cherub, and fill thine hand with coals of fire from between the cherubims, and scatter them over the city. And he went in in my sight" (Ezekiel 10:1,2).

A cherubic chariot and the angel of the covenant were the instruments of judgment. While the fiery coals of judgment were being scattered, the chariot of God and the covenant angel stood over the house of God.

I tremble as I write about what Ezekiel saw next because it concerns our day. The chariot and the angel had come to the east gate to take up and remove the glory of God from his house. The cloud, once in the holy of holies, was moving now to the outer court. This signifies first that the rent veil made it possible for all

believers to experience God's glory and grace. But here
we see the glory of God moving slowly to the outer court
for one last burst of brightness and revelation before it
departed. "And the cloud filled the inner court. Then
the glory of the Lord went up from the cherub, and
stood over the threshold of the house; and the house
was filled with the cloud, and the court was full of the
brightness of the Lord's glory" (Ezekiel 10:3,4).

This is why I tremble: the glory of the Lord is being
mightily manifested now for the last time. There will
be one final, glorious harvest. Soon it will depart and
judgment will fall—beginning in the house of the
Lord. The glory is right now at the threshold of the
church, and there is shining forth the most brilliant
call to repentance and holiness mankind has ever
received.

While the glory hovered over the threshold of God's
house, the angel took coals of fire and scattered them
in the house. These are the consuming coals of fire
that cleansed the lips of Isaiah. Overcomers are going
to be cleansed and purified before judgment falls
through a revelation of the power of the Cross. The revelation of holiness by faith will be accompanied by a
final outshining of the Lord's glory.

Moreover, while the glory tarried, an awesome sight
was seen in the heavens. Celestial beings appeared
"full of eyes." "And their whole body, and their backs,
and their hands, and their wings, and the wheels, were
full of eyes round about" (Ezekiel 10:12).

This symbolizes God's final heart-searching before
judgment. The eyes of the Lord, and many they be,
search God's people even now, exposing hidden sin,
shining light on all hidden works of darkness, and taking record of all deeds unknown except to His eyes.
There is nothing covered that shall not be revealed.
There are penetrating eyes in God's glory. Isaiah said,

"Jerusalem is ruined, and Judah is fallen: because their tongue and their doings are against the Lord, to provoke the eyes of his glory" (Isaiah 3:8). David said, "His eyes behold the nations" (Psalm 66:7).

David saw the same vision Ezekiel saw. He wrote, "The Lord is in his holy temple, the Lord's throne is in heaven: his eyes behold, his eyelids try, the children of men" (Psalm 11:4).

Every believer, every minister of the gospel is right now under trial by His flaming eyes. Thank God, the glory has not yet departed. But our God has taken His judgmental position in the firmament over the earth; His glory now shines in all its celestial splendor and power, calling all overcomers to the laver for cleansing. Time is fast running out; the cherubic chariot and the covenant angel will soon be commanded to do their frightful task of removing God's glory from His house.

I know in my heart that the Holy Spirit is doing His final work of conviction. How long will He continue to deal with a stubborn, lukewarm, playful people? How many times has the blessed Spirit of God warned His people to forsake their sinful ways? Not a single Christian reading these words can deny the terrible probings, the shattering conviction of the Spirit in his life. It is because God is calling out the bride He will give His Son. It is to be a spotless bride, pure, holy, separated, and free of all other loves.

Do you think for one moment Christ will take to Himself a contaminated, lust-bound bride? Will ministers of His gospel be in that bride who continue in their adultery? Will He come for those who pollute their garments with filthy pornography, who sneak into X-rated theaters, who secretly flood their minds with eroticism? No!

Oh, my precious Lord—what a terrible day that will be when suddenly the cherubims and the covenant angel are called to attention and return to God's throne, taking with them all of His glory. Out from the east gate it will depart, never to return until God's kingdom rules supreme. "When they stood, these stood; and when they were lifted up, these lifted up themselves also: for the spirit of the living creature was in them. Then the glory of the Lord departed from off the threshold of the house, and stood over the cherubims" (Ezekiel 10:17,18).

What happened when the glory of the Lord departed from the house of God at Shiloh? "But go ye now unto my place which was in Shiloh, where I set my name at the first, and see what I did to it for the wickedness of my people Israel. And now, because ye have done all these works, saith the Lord, and I spake unto you, rising up early and speaking, but ye heard not; and I called you, but ye answered not; therefore will I do unto this house, which is called by my name, wherein ye trust, and unto the place which I gave to you and to your fathers, as I have done to Shiloh. And I will cast you out of my sight, as I have cast out all your brethren, even the whole seed of Ephraim" (Jeremiah 7:12-15). Ichabod followed, which means, "The glory has departed." Beloved, there is so little time for God's people to repent, for the ministry to be purified, for a forsaking of all idols and ungodliness. Ezekiel saw our day, and he was astonished beyond words that the glory of God would depart and stand over the cherubims in the heavens.

I believe the glory of God has already departed from many ministries and their leaders. Multitudes of Christians are now under the influence of lying spirits, and they have been lulled to sleep in their sins. Ichabod has been written upon their thresholds, and they will be fuel for the fires of judgment.

Servant of God—if there is ever to be a time you will

get free, it had better be now. Your days are numbered; you must cry out to God in contrition, and let the Spirit of God probe your hidden areas and give you power to forsake your secret sins. Otherwise, the glory of God will forever depart your life, and you will fall under the cloud of Shiloh.

It is impossible for overcomers to lose the glory of God. But Paul makes it clear they will be seated with Christ in heavenly places; and what will be fiery wrath on the compromisers, will be instant glorification for the righteous. As it is, the only reason the glory now tarries at the threshold of the church is because the Lord is calling out and calling together all His overcomers. I see that glory; it has touched my life, opened my eyes, and led me to the true body of Christ who also has come to it.

Soon, the only glory that will remain before judgment will be in the hearts of the overcomers. All others will be bankrupt. All the foolish virgins will have nothing for their lamps, and they will be left out.

Refining and Exposure

Malachi prophesied, "He shall sit as a refiner and purifier of silver: and he shall purify the sons of Levi, and purge them as gold and silver, that they may offer unto the Lord an offering in righteousness" (Malachi 3:3).

When a man of God hides sin in his heart, nothing he does is accepted by God. Souls may be saved in spite of him, because the Word itself bears its own fruit. But God makes it clear in this prophecy that He is sovereignly going to shut down every man of God, put him in His refining fire, and burn up all that is not holy and acceptable to Him. Those who refuse the purging fire will be cast aside as salt that has lost its savor.

Much of what the church glories in now is an abomination in the eyes of God. But none of the hype, none of the foolishness, none of the lightness, none of the double standards, none of the flirting and sensuality will survive the coming fires.

God is also going to dispatch a huge flock of telltale birds to sit on the window of every room and place in which ministers and laymen indulge in secret sin, and they will tell it to the world. "For a bird of the air shall carry the voice, and that which hath wings shall tell the matter" (Ecclesiastes 10:20). Jesus said, "For there is nothing hid, which shall not be manifested; neither was any thing kept secret, but that it should come abroad" (Mark 4:22).

God will protect the reputation and ministry of that one who rushes to the Cross and to death of self. All heaven goes in motion for the servant of the Lord who truly repents and who, by faith, comes to the light to have his evil deeds exposed to Christ. God has a body of men like that, men who have come through white-hot fires of temptation and who, at the very point of failure and despair, ran to His sheltering arms for deliverance. These are those who now hate this sin more than others. They have experienced its horrors, its bondage, its vicious demands; and they cannot stand idly by and watch other men of God fall into the same trap. I can always tell by the way a man preaches whether or not he has rolled in death on his sin and come out the other side to resurrection power. There is such glory, such amazing peace, such rest on the victory side of Jordan—you can tell it when you see it in a man.

God Judged David for Adultery

I believe David grieved God's heart more than any other man on earth, including Judas. God loved this gracious, holy poet and had granted to him a glorious anointing. God gave David a good name among his people and in all heathen nations. His name was synonymous with righteousness. His loving heart had to be the talk of heaven because of his deep yearnings for the heart of God. His tears were diamonds in the Lord's eyes.

But this godly prince of Israel was hiding a dark secret. He had committed adultery with the beautiful Bathsheba. To cover his sin, he had to stoop to lying and murder. Having ordered her husband's execution by the hand of the enemy, David quietly took Bathsheba into his royal household to be his wife. It looked like a very neat cover-up, with only a few close friends knowing the full extent of his crime.

There is a profound difference between Samson and David. Samson had in him "a spirit of adultery." He indulged his lust time and again with no conviction whatsoever. In one night, he could fight God's battle and win a great victory, only to end up in bed with a harlot. It was a way of life to him. He loved God, but he had no intention of giving up his desire for strange women. Consequently, God had to silence him, lest he bring even greater reproach on the name of Jehovah.

David's adultery was "an occasion." It was a one-time indulgence, committed in a time of momentary weakness. He hated adultery; he had cried against it in his songs and in his messages to the people. David, after his sin, was still zealous for the holiness of God.

Certainly David's sin made all of heaven weep. When Saul fell to the enemy, David lamented, "How are the mighty fallen!...as though he had not been anointed" (2 Samuel 1:19-21). I believe David's sin caused the angels to lament, "How the mighty man with God has fallen in the midst of battle. The beauty of Israel is slain upon thy high places" (2 Samuel 1:19,27).

Bathsheba still sits in the pew. She is not the paint-

42

ed, gaudy, streetwalker Delilah. No such ungodly woman would have been a temptation to the pious David. Bathsheba was not a harlot; she was a faithful, God-fearing wife of a man in God's army. She was apparently a very godly woman, one who practiced the Jewish purity rites, one who had a Solomon in her genes. Solomon could have never grown up to be the man of God he became without the godly heritage of a spiritual mother.

What unthinkable consequences when a godly man and a spiritual woman bare their souls to one another, without their mates present. David communed with Bathsheba—and it was then he was so drawn to her. Abigail, his wife, was also a beautiful woman. It had to be more than Bathsheba's beauty that caused David to risk his kingdom. He saw God in her. She spoke like no other woman he had known. She shared his love for God, his compassion for hurting people. She was not materialistic like other women; she was not promiscuous; she was pure and innocent. He seemed so at peace, so natural with her. It was as though he had known her all his life. To lay with her seemed so right, almost spiritual. No doubt he even entertained thoughts that God had brought her into his life to help him become a better man of God. Somehow, it would turn out right, because there was no deep sense of grieving God.

She had been blinded by his reputation and his love for God. Perhaps she thought he could do no wrong. There is no mention of a protest from her. She had not seduced him; but now that they had bared their souls to one another, she clung to that occasion. She, no doubt, left his presence thinking to herself, "He really is a man of God. Nobody knows him now better than I do. His tears touched me. Nobody knows what he's been through. I've touched something in him nobody else has touched. I made him come alive. I can help him be a better leader. I know we took matters in our own hands, but God will see us through."

How do I know these things are true? Because human nature never changes. David and Bathsheba said and thought the very same things adulterers say and think today. The games they play never change; the excuses, the lying, the cover-ups all fall into the same categories.

Most ministers I know who have had an affair tell me they were attracted by the spirituality of the woman. "It just happened," they confess. "We were somehow drawn to each other. She met a need in my life; she was one with me in the spiritual realm. It was really not as physical as it was spiritual." I have yet to meet an adulterer who was not convinced the relationship was spiritual more than physical. Some pray and read their Bibles together, hopefully provoking one another to go deeper in God. It somehow helps ease the pricking of the conscience.

"The Thing David Did Displeased the Lord" (2 Samuel 11:27)

God's displeasure—what an awesome thought! How wrong to look beyond the judgments of God to the time Bathsheba became queen and gave birth to Solomon. It is true, this is one of the most hopeful expressions of God's grace in all His Word. But too many think to themselves, "The consequences can't be that bad. After all, God forgave David, let him continue as king, and even made their son of the royal seed of Christ."

What about God's judgment on their adultery? There is the tragedy of the death of their illegitimate baby, "that the Lord struck, until it was very sick" (2 Samuel 12:15). Poor Bathsheba, she was the one who suf-

. She lost the husband of her youth, lost a
s child, and bore the greatest reproach. Too
n, men of God think only of their suffering as the
result of adultery and forget the pain of the one they
harmed.

There is the matter of "giving great occasion to the
enemies of the Lord to blaspheme" (2 Samuel 12:14). There
is God's terrifying threat to "raise up evil against thee
out of thine own house" (2 Samuel 12:11). He would be
publicly exposed and shamed. God said to him, "You
did it secretly; but I will do this thing before all Israel,
and before the sun" (2 Samuel 12:12).

God declared adultery to be "a sin against the
Lord—a despising of His commandment—a despising
of the Lord Himself" (2 Samuel 12:9,13). I believe David
found forgiveness and was fully restored because he
recognized his sin as "a sin against the Lord." He had
not sinned only against his family, or against God's
people, or against society at large. It was a sin against
God. The terror of that had gripped his soul. His sorrow was not in being caught or exposed—but in that he
had sinned against His beloved Lord.

God's threat to raise up evil in David's own household is revealed in the very next chapter. Amnon, his
grandson, raped Tamar, his granddaughter (2 Samuel
13). Absalom, his beloved son, rebelled and threatened
his very life. Absalom was killed and David ended up
wailing profusely, "O my son Absalom, my son, my son
Absalom! Would God I had died in your place, O Absalom, my son, my son" (2 Samuel 18:33).

Don't Be Fooled by What You See

Saints of God, don't look at the way things appear.
Servants of God cheat on their wives, then go on with
new wives, apparently still enjoying God's blessings!
Not so! You do not see or hear of God's judgment on

them. You know nothing of the sleepless nights, the despair and sorrow that floods in on them. To live under God's displeasure is a burden few can bear. To have the heavens shut and end up ministering in the flesh leaves its mark on men. Little by little, their influence wanes, their following dwindles. People may smile at them, but there is an insurmountable loss of respect. Those who live and preach as adulterers minister death and not life. What they say is tainted by their evil deeds. They are heard only by the ear, and not the heart.

The only message with power is that which is preached from a pure heart, by men with clean hands. All else is sounding brass and tinkling cymbals. God will not speak to a man or woman living in sin; He closes the heavens to those who break and flaunt His commandments. So what they preach has to come out of their own hearts and minds and can only be man-centered. They have no searing, scorching word from God that drives men to their knees. They strike no fear to divided hearts and compromisers. Their thunder has been silenced by the evil charms of an adulterous woman.

We don't have to go about with eyes full of lust—we don't have to be looking at all—but Satan will always try to use a supposed lack in our lives to snare us in an evil relationship. Those kinds of relationships may be justified and continued for years on the grounds that we are all the better for it. Both may provoke each other to pray more and go deeper in God. But it is still sin!

The mate always knows. There is a strange wall that is erected, and nothing but honesty can ever penetrate it. There is an aloofness, a holding back, something you can't put your finger on, but you know something is really wrong.

A man of God can stand in the pulpit and preach

with all his might, then give his heart and time to an adulterous relationship. Then, if he is a true man of God, he weeps over what he has done. He feels his heart going out in the wrong direction; he feels Satan breathing down his neck, trying to wreck his ministry; and he cries out to God to be free of the attraction. How deeply it becomes embedded in the soul! What an ocean of tears is shed in sorrow of heart, because there seems to be no way out.

He hears in the deepest of his soul the taunting cry, "You are a phony! You preach against this very thing! You are hooked just like any common drug addict! You preach freedom from sin, and you are enslaved! Liar!"

There is the constant fear of exposure and, worst of all, the hounding fear of bringing reproach on God's name. There is the fear of ending up like Samson, stripped and shelved by God—or even worse, judgment by death.

The man of God caught in this kind of snare will walk his room at night, begging God for cleansing. His heart will yearn for the day he can once again look God and the world in the eye and proclaim, "I am clean! I am pure! I am free!"

Oh, the broken promises, the lies. What appears to be a victory only ends in defeat. Just when you think it is dead, it comes back again in greater force. Then it is realized that only a true death at the Cross can deliver from its hold.

Many a great man of God has come this way to the Cross—broken down, helpless, having broken every promise, weary of grieving God and ministering under a lie. God has used that crisis to roll in death on everything in that man's life and raise him to resurrection life and glorious freedom.

There can be no deliverance from an adulterous attraction outside of total death at the Cross. Cry a river of tears, try to kill it on your own, suppress it any way you can—it will still be there. And, it will eventually destroy both of you. You will go back to it; you will always have that lingering memory erupting unexpectedly.

Take my warning—O man of God! You are not above this kind of sin.

No One in the Congregation Will Escape God's Passion Against Adultery and Divorce

The people of God have winked at adultery and have accepted divorce as inevitable in these troubled times. I have preached in churches in which one-third to one-half of the congregation was divorced; some, two and three times.

God sees what we are afraid to even think or speak aloud. He sees the cancerous spreading of unfaithfulness, the breaking up of Christian homes, the lust for new mates, the heartbreak and sorrow that now plagues churches throughout the land.

When pastors become patsies about divorce, they open the floodgates to a tidal wave of marriage break-ups. When there is no prophet of God in the pulpit to reveal God's hatred of divorce to them, when no one challenges their self-centeredness, when no one tells them the truth about the horrible consequences of divorce and the judgment of God—it's no wonder they split up so readily.

I believe in the grace of God, but I also believe in His government. The divorced can find forgiveness—that is beyond question. But who is standing up to tell them that God's government must go on, and they must come under it? I know of few ministers who have preached a sermon on the judgmental consequences of divorce.

It was grace that clothed Adam; it was government

that drove him out of Eden. His coat of skin was evidence of grace; the flaming sword, the solemn fulfillment of government. Why did God drive a forgiven man out of the garden into a future of turmoil? Grace forgives; but the wheels of God's government roll on in all their terrible consequences. Adam was perfectly forgiven, but his sin produced its own terrible results. His guilt was removed, but not the sweat of his brow. He was pardoned, but he was sent to live among thorns. Grace fully pardons, but what is sown must be reaped. Pardon doesn't change the nature of the crop sown.

Moses spoke unadvisedly with his lips. God's governmental decree prohibited his entrance into the promised land. God's love and grace took him to Pisgah and tenderly buried him, but he never came into the fullness of Canaan.

David fell under the blinding power of lust. God's grace declared to him, "The Lord hath put away thy sin." That was absolute grace; he was perfectly forgiven! But all the while, God's wheels of government kept turning and the sword of judgment was drawn. The baby died; Absalom rebelled; Amnon raped Tamar; David was chased over the hills again like a fugitive.

The manifestation of God in government is not being preached from many pulpits today. All we are hearing is God manifested in grace, love, and mercy. God is merciful and gracious, longsuffering, and abundant in goodness, keeping mercy for thousands, forgiving iniquity and transgression and sin. But He also declares He will not overlook or clear the guilty, visiting the iniquity of the fathers upon the children and upon the children's children, unto the third and fourth generation. [See Exodus 34:6,7]

In a time of deep spiritual declension, the Holy Spirit calls for bold, drastic steps to stem the tide of immorality. Ezra was so shocked by the iniquity among

God's people throughout Judah and Jerusalem, he cried out, "O my God, I am ashamed and blush to lift up my face to thee, my God: for our iniquities are increased over our head, and our trespass is grown up unto the heavens" (Ezra 9:6).

Ezra saw abomination in the house of God from one end to the other. God's chosen people had become unclean by joining affinity with the worldly and mixing the holy seed with the people of heathen lands. Not even the priests and Levites were separated, having committed abominations just like the congregation. They had been divorcing at will and not a voice was raised in protest. They were marrying and remarrying at will, even to those whom God said they were forbidden to marry.

Ezra did not reach out to them with compassion and tolerance. Instead, "He tore his garment and mantle, and plucked off the hair of his head and beard, and sat down confounded" (Ezra 9:3). This dear man of God fell on his knees, spread out his hands to God, and prayed for "a little space" to repent and find grace. "He ate no bread, nor did he drink water; for he mourned because of the transgression of them that had been carried away" (Ezra 10:6).

What about our congregations being carried away by adultery and divorce? Is this the time to call for tolerance and acceptance of what is truly hateful in God's eyes? Where are those who share the grief of God's heart over the backsliding, the cheating, the tearing apart of our homes? Every true man of God ought to be on his face, crying out to God as Ezra, mourning over the evil flooding God's people, repenting and calling their people to repentance.

Ezra demanded radical steps to restore righteousness. He said to the transgressors, "Ye have transgressed, and have taken strange wives, to increase the sin of Israel" (Ezra 10:10). Some of them had children by those foreign wives. They had settled down and had established homes. But Ezra came into the picture, demanding they "separate from the people of the land, and from the strange wives" (Ezra 10:11). They asked for time to obey God "because we are many that have transgressed in this thing" (Ezra 10:13). A nationwide separation followed. It was a radical breaking away from an evil course and a return to the Lord's commandments and good pleasure. The actions "turned away the fierce wrath of God."

Had we stood in Ezra's place, we would have opted for compassion. "For the children's sake," we would have said, "let things continue as they are. God is loving and merciful. The children's welfare is more important than God's commandments! God is not that kind!"

We would have excused our dearest friends. We would have excused the high-paying members of the church. We would have looked the other way when dealing with the famous and the powerful.

God was a God of love in the Old Testament, as much as He is a God of love today. God's radical demand for separation during Ezra's time was an act of love of the truest kind. He was trying to save a remnant from total destruction, to give them a nail in the holy place; to lighten their eyes; and to revive them. [See Ezra 9:8]

This is not a time for tolerance of sin and disobedience. It is a time to take a stand for the holiness and honor of almighty God. I blame the pulpits for the lackadaisical attitude in the church about divorce. When writers of some of our most popular religious books leave their wives and remarry, without even an explanation, is it any wonder young Christians are weakened in their attitude about divorce and remarriage?

It should be enough for us that God says He hates divorce. Rather than build walls of protection for marriage on the power of that holy Word, we spend our time looking for loopholes.

God has soundly rebuked me for preaching an all-too-condescending, forgiving message about divorce and remarriage. I felt the agony of all the innocent parties, the loneliness of those abandoned by adulterous mates, the isolation and guilt of those already divorced and remarried who still are deeply devoted to the Lord. But in preaching love, hope, and forgiveness to them, many others who were plotting to leave their mates found solace and even encouragement. The thought emerged, "It may be wrong, but I'll take the plunge then throw myself on the mercy of God. Others found grace—so will I."

I don't have all the answers, but I do know I've heard from God about what is coming. Those Christians who have been warned, those who outright reject God's hatred toward divorce, those who build a case to justify their evil deeds—they will never again find a place of rest and peace in the Lord. Their new marriages will bring them only more disaster and turmoil. The blessing of God will not return, and what they thought would be the answer to their needs will become a thorn in their side. God has had enough of it, and He is going to send canker and rust to eat the life out of all that is abominable to Him.

My purpose in this book is not to berate those who are innocent victims of divorce, who are now remarried and seeking the Lord. Nor am I putting down ministers victimized by a hopeless situation. God knows how to protect, honor, and make useful those who are innocent. God is very merciful to the repentant. My purpose, under God's hand, is to put the fear of God into those who think they can walk out on their commitment and take up with someone else—without suffering the wrath and swift judgment of a holy God. His

52

wrath has already broken forth in the church against such offenders, and that wrath will soon be evident to all. As He said to David, He is saying to us, "You did it in secret, but your judgment will be open to the eyes of the world."

May God give us ministers of His gospel who will quit trying to accommodate the weaknesses of God's people and who will get to know God's heart—until they are willing to stand in the gap and save the people from their sins.

God, put Your holy fear in us and give us a new reverence for Your divine government and righteous judgments.

Chapter 3

"My People Have Set Them Up Idols"

"And they set them up idols...as did the heathen" (2 Kings 17:11-15).

The world is about to burn and its foundations shaken by the almighty hand of God, and Christians sit nonchalantly before their television idol, wasting precious time. How Satan and the hoards of hell must laugh with glee at the sight of millions of Christians sitting before his Babylonian idiot box, losing their zeal for God.

Satan is succeeding through television in a way not possible by any other kind of demonic invasion. Through that speaking idol, he can accomplish in this generation what he accomplished in Eden. He once again is tempting and enticing with the same three seductions: pride of life, lust of the eyes, and lust of the flesh. Television makes all three seductions possible.

Twenty-five years ago television was rather innocent and harmless. There was wholesome family entertainment, and high moral standards were honored. Each broadcasting day was closed with a sermonette and a prayer. Few of God's people were condemned by it, except for the many wasted hours. In the past few years that has all changed, and television is now not innocent, not wholesome, and not worthy of the moral standard of a devoted lover of the Lord Jesus Christ.

The spirit of the world and of Antichrist now controls secular television. "For all that is in the world, the lust of the flesh, and the lust of the eyes, and the pride of life, is not of the Father, but is of the world" (1 John 2:16). And whosoever loves the world and its things, "the love of the Father is not in him" (1 John 2:15).

God has put it in my heart to sound His trumpet against all the idols in the lives and homes of God's dear people until it can be said of us all, "We will walk within our houses with a perfect heart. We will set no wicked thing before our eyes...it shall not get a hold on us" (Psalm 101:2,3). Some, when reading this chapter, will have to say, "I didn't know television had become such an evil idol! I didn't know God felt so angered by it! I didn't know it has become Satan's most powerful weapon in these last days against the people and the church of God!"

The overcomers ought to move quickly to cast the abomination aside and escape this terrible snare of Satan. Once the true lover of Jesus hears the clear Word of the Lord against such idols, he ought to obey and be purged of sin. On the other hand, the majority of Christians and ministers will scoff. They will dig up Paul's argument about idols being nothing. But they will refuse to hear Paul's terrible thundering about the demonic spirit behind the idols.

This message is only for those who tremble at the Word of God and for true believers who are open to the present-day work of Holy Ghost conviction. The Holy Spirit is right now convicting His body about committing spiritual adultery with this technical idol, as well as all the other idols He is exposing. Thousands of praying Christians have been convicted of having this accursed thing in their homes, and they have obeyed the Spirit's command to throw it out. It is gone from my home, and I am led to speak forth what the Word of God has shown me about His impatience against it. Certainly the bride of Christ ought not pollute herself with such wicked fornication.

I believe Satan has taken full possession of secular television, and it has become his most powerful stronghold. I believe that demonic principalities and powers are now in full control of much of the programming on television, including the horrible erotic commercials.

The Sodomites Are in the House

When I was praying about this message, I heard ringing in my spiritual ears, "The sodomites are in the house! The sodomites are in the house!" I knew it was God speaking to me about the wickedness of television. I remembered the story of Lot and the visiting angels he entertained overnight. The Sodomites from all over Sodom surrounded Lot's house, trying to break down the door, get in, and attack the visiting angels. But the angelic men blinded the Sodomites and they never did get in.

But the sodomites are in now—in our homes. And we are now the blinded ones. Homosexual writers, actors, and producers flaunt their evil ways right before our eyes; and admit it or not, you and all in your home are under a demonic sodomite attack.

Some imply that violence on television is not a key issue—but I say it is. God hates violence; He once destroyed the earth because of it. "And God said unto Noah, The end of all flesh is come before me; for the earth is filled with violence through them; and, behold, I will destroy them with the earth" (Genesis 6:13).

There is coming soon to this nation an unbelievable outbreak of violence that no one would dare believe could be so wild, wicked, and widespread. You can see the growing storm of violence developing on television even now. Wrestlers who once faked blood with dye capsules are now paid big money to cut themselves and each other. Thousands flock to see the bleeding wrestlers wallow in blood. Now it's being televised and multitudes of Americans are becoming bloodthirsty. We are getting very close to the spirit of Rome, with its lions and gladiators and bloodshed.

God's anger burns against the endless and bloody show of violence. How can the Lord keep His hand and Spirit upon Christians who give their silent consent to it by viewing it. God spoke powerfully to me about His wrath against it when I still had the idol in my home. While watching a violent, five-man team murder and maim, the Holy Spirit came upon me, causing me to tremble. I heard Him say to me in no uncertain terms that He would not let me keep my anointing if I kept watching it—and that I must see my television as an animated idol of Satan and cast it out once and for all. I was made to know there would be no full revelation, no open heaven, no continuous unction, no fulfilling of His perfect will if I disobeyed and continued squandering precious time before that shrine of hell. The day I obeyed and cast it out, I fell on my face before God and wept for hours. The release was so glorious! I realized what a terrible hold this satanic snare had on me and on most of God's people.

I warn Christians now about television, and they find it nearly impossible to give it up. Can you? I see Christians so powerfully addicted to television, and I weep over their blindness. Even the holiest of God's people have been enslaved by it, but they can't admit it. The time has come wherein the Holy Spirit is revealing the horror of this idol so clearly, no overcomer will be able to sit before it and still be in close communion with Christ.

The addiction of Christians to television really alarms me. Truly dedicated believers will agree with all I say about impending judgment, about the music of devils in God's house, about adultery in the church, and about spiritual deadness among the Lord's people. But no one dares touch their beloved television. In sharing the message of this trumpet call, I discovered, to my dismay, that television has become one of the most sensitive issues of all. My dearest friends tell me, "I know what you have heard is from the Lord. I sense the Spirit's anointing on your warnings. There is a certain sound that touches something deep in me. But this thing about television becoming an idol—I can't buy that. That's just something God is dealing with you about. It's not a message for the church or for mature Christians." To see so many precious children of God desensitized and defensive about television honestly scares me. What kind of mystical hold does it have on this age? Why does the family of Jesus Christ find it so hard to give up? It makes me know all the more that the Holy Spirit has truly called me to warn about its danger. We need to hear the piercing words of John the Baptist once again, "Bring forth therefore fruits worthy of repentance" (Luke 3:8).   Paul, preacher of grace, preached the same thing. "But shewed first unto them of Damascus, and at Jerusalem, and throughout all the coasts of Judea, and then to the Gentiles, that they should repent and turn to God, and do works meet for repentance" (Acts 26:20). Works do not save us; they are evidence of grace.

I believe every Christian reading this will soon have to choose or abort the fullness of the Spirit. Ezekiel warned, "They are separated from me through their idols" (Ezekiel 14:5). Not because I say so, but because it will become so vile, so corrupt, even the most carnal Christians will recognize Satan's overruling hand in it.

The Accursed Thing and the Anger of God

"But the children of Israel committed a trespass in the accursed thing" (Joshua 7:1).

Just before he died, Moses had warned the children of Israel, "Thou shalt not bring an abomination into thine house, lest thou be a cursed thing like it: but thou shalt utterly detest it, and thou shalt utterly abhor it; for it is a cursed thing" (Deuteronomy 7:26).

That same warning was given to Israel by Joshua just before the battle of Jericho. He warned, "And ye, in any wise keep yourselves from the accursed thing, lest ye make yourselves accursed, when ye take of the accursed thing, and make the camp of Israel a curse, and trouble it" (Joshua 6:18).

A soldier by the name of Achan "took of the accursed thing: and the anger of the Lord was kindled against the children of Israel" (Joshua 7:1). He kept for himself and took home a Babylonish garment, two hundred shekels of silver, and a wedge of gold of fifty shekels weight. He admitted, "I coveted them, and took them; and, behold, they are hid in my tent" (Joshua 7:21).

What is this abominable, accursed thing God so despises—so much so that He abandoned Israel for even touching it? God hated it so, He permitted Israel to flee before their enemies because one man had the accursed thing in his dwelling. Was it not just a coat and a few hundred dollars worth of silver and gold? What could be so abominable and accursed about that? It was the same kind of silver and gold the Israelites traded with.

It was not the things in themselves, it was what they represented. They were abominations because they represented the spirit and passion of evil and violent men. These things were accursed because of the great temptations they represented, with the potential to corrupt the morals of God's people. All along the way God was protecting a holy, peculiar people—trying to keep them from coveting the things and the ways of the heathen.

I take it very seriously when I read, "And the anger of the Lord was kindled against Israel. Israel hath sinned, and they have also transgressed my covenant...for they have even taken of the accursed thing...and lied...and they have put it even among their own stuff" (Joshua 7:1,11).

Because of the accursed thing among them, they could not stand before their enemies, "but turned their backs before their enemies, because they were accursed: neither will I be with you any more, except ye destroy the accursed from among you" (Joshua 7:12).

Those are the very same words I heard from God. "If you value My sweet presence, if you want a high hedge about you, if you want to stand tall against the enemies of your soul, get rid of that accursed idol in your home." That is why we got rid of our television sets. Not because of some legalistic hang-up—never! Busting TV sets can save no one. There is no merit to it, and I am not with those who pile up TV sets in public meetings and smash them. I believe in justification by faith alone; we are not talking about salvation. Removing this idol removes one of the greatest hindrances to the fullness of Christ and an open heaven of glorious revelation. It is not a work of righteousness and can add nothing to the grace of God. It is simply an act of loving obedience to the Word of God.

To me, it is beyond question that secular television has become the abominable, cursed thing in Christian homes. It is animated by the spirit of Satan—it is the modern Baal. It puts believers in the seat of the scornful; it puts before our eyes that which is evil; it is "to provoke the eyes of God's glory." God's name is taken in vain, marriage and fidelity is scorned, religion is satirized, and holiness is jeered. Satan's aim is to get the whole world, including Christians, to laugh at things holy and sacred. Even situation comedies mock morality; and all that is pure, honest, and Christian is ridiculed. How sad that Christians laugh at what should be making us weep. How dare we continue to drink in that which grieves and infuriates the Holy Spirit! Will we not be judged for it?

Whether we want to accept it or not, I am totally convinced that secular television has come under the devil's control, and God is incensed against it. When the Lord's anger against it is fully known, and the Holy Spirit tells us to get rid of it—we had better obey. I think we are already seeing the tragic results, even in the best of Christian homes, of the curse of this idol. This trumpet call is a part of the Holy Spirit's warning to overcomers. I am so convinced God considers it accursed, I am emboldened to say to all overcomers— Get rid of it now!—lest He leave us to our stubborn covetousness (Joshua 7:12).

I hear the Spirit say, "Up, sanctify yourselves.... There is an accursed thing in the midst of thee...thou canst not stand before thine enemies, until ye take away the accursed thing from among you" (Joshua 7:13). God called it "folly in Israel" (Joshua 7:15).

It is significant that the prophets called idol worship folly. The prophets described an idol as "that which does not profit" (Jeremiah 16:19). They were called "delectable things that do not profit." There is a familiar ring in their lamentations over the idolatry of Israel. "They set them up idols...as did the heathen...and wrought wicked things to provoke the Lord to anger; for they served idols...they became vain...following after the heathen" (2 Kings 17:11-15).

We are no longer under the curse of the Law, but sin and disobedience must always be judged. There is still a moral law we dare not ignore. Judgment begins in the house of God, and those who still tremble at the Word of God will hear what the Spirit is saying about this matter.

Our Idols Have Withheld The Latter Rain

"Thou hast polluted the land with thy whoredoms and with thy wickedness. Therefore the showers have been withholden, and there hath been no latter rain" (Jeremiah 3:2,3).

The latter rain has been falling since Pentecost, but God is withholding it for many in these times because of wickedness and going after idols.

Certainly there are areas where the rain is falling, but the greater picture of the church and the Christian's home is one of dryness. The showers are being withheld because of whoredom—spiritual idolatry.

God's grief is that His children are dying of thirst when His desire is to send them overflowing floods on dry ground—to send waters to swim in. Our Christian homes should be constantly enjoying His soft rain as on new mown grass, the gentle falling of His Holy Spirit upon us throughout the day. Instead, a blaring television disturbs the tranquility with filth that no Christian home should permit under its roof. Our churches should be overflowing with the living waters that come from His throne. We should be drinking to the full, bringing life to barren grounds. But we are not getting the latter rain because it is being withheld—and it will not rain again until the abomination is taken away. We come into God's presence with our minds preoccupied with mental visions of seductive programs.

62

The rain is falling in our home now that the accursed thing is gone. The rain is falling afresh on my ministry. I've been flooded in my soul by the waters of life. It began the day I tore down **all** my idols: the spirit of adultery, ungodly music, television, and all else that was of no profit. I believe what Isaiah said, "And the loftiness of man shall be bowed down, and the haughtiness of men shall be made low: and the Lord alone shall be exalted in that day. And the idols he shall utterly abolish" (Isaiah 2:17,18).

The Religious Crowd Will Cry, "Legalism!"

A staff member of mine was raised in a very strict home where television was forbidden. The children were not even permitted to go to a neighbor's house to watch it. He tells of the terrible abuse he and his brother had heaped on them because of the stand their "holiness" dad took. They were laughed at, ridiculed, and mocked.

When he married and had children, he promised them they would always have a television set in their home—so they would never have to take abuse from anyone. But the Holy Spirit began to convict him as he watched his boy getting rebellious, acting out scenes he was picking up from viewing television.

He came to me while I was in the middle of writing this chapter and tearfully poured out his heart. "Do you know where all the criticism came from when we were children?" he asked. "From the devil's crowd," I quickly answered. "No sir! It came from the church people, choir members, other kids in the church. It came from other ministers who made fun of my father's 'legalism.'"

He doesn't care now; God has delivered him and his family from all fear; and the idol is gone. He has a new respect for his deceased preacher dad. "He was right all the time," he says.

Where will most criticism come from about the message of this chapter? From prostitutes, addicts, gamblers and criminal types? From liberal ministers and high church laymen? No! It will come from evangelical, Pentecostal, Baptist preachers who will write it all off as legalism. I will be put in the same category as the rock record smashers and book burners. They will say, "It is not an idol just because he says so. It offers too much good to get rid of it. The author is trying to impose his convictions on all believers."

It doesn't matter to me anymore. But it does cause grief when the ungodly say Amen and the believers scoff.

Paul said the idol is nothing, the meat offered to it is nothing, but he warned of the spirit behind it. The TV box is nothing; it is an inanimate piece of furniture. But there is a spirit behind it, animating it, controlling it, influencing the mind toward evil. Certainly it is possible for a man of God to animate it with spiritual power, but that ought to be directed toward the lost and does not require my viewing it.

What About the Elderly And the Shut-Ins?

I do not wish to condemn the elderly and the shut-ins who get their spiritual encouragement from television pastors and evangelists. Television services offer a ray of hope and blessing to many who cannot go to church. Yet there are some questions that need to be asked in this area. What was it like before television? It's only been the last thirty years that sets have become so available. Is God so weak, so neglectful that He cannot fill the void? Have we forgotten His promise to keep us in our old age? "And even to your old age I am he; and even to hoar hairs will I carry you: I have made, and I will bear; even I will carry, and will deliver you" (Isaiah 46:4).

Nothing has so destroyed the prayer life of the old-time mothers of Zion as television. Those dear old grandmothers and grandfathers who spent hours praying, interceeding—many of them are now feeding their souls on the devil's garbage.

I cringe when I hear Christians say, "Well, you can't spend all your time praying, reading your Bible, studying, and just reading spiritual books. Everybody needs relaxation." This kind of talk only reveals how far we have strayed from spiritual paths. The true worshipper knows no better relaxation than a few hours beholding the love of Jesus and drinking in His beauty—daily. How can a child of God be bored if truly walking and living in the Spirit? Any shut-in that can hear television can hear Bible tapes. What better comfort to the old, the sick, and the infirm? Is it better to face eternity drenched in God's uplifting Word or in the filthy, unsatisfying waters of the world's cisterns?

You say I am not compassionate, not considerate of the elderly and the shut-ins? That I am taking from them their one last source of entertainment? No! Millions of elderly saints have gone into eternity over the years without such a crutch. I don't wish for them to fail in their latter years—like the dear old missionary lady I know who, after fifty years of winning souls, now sits for hours in front of her television, without a trace of spiritual life left in her. Her children hate what it has done to their once saintly mother.

Our thinking has become so twisted, our moral standards so crushed, I don't think we have the spiritual fortitude to take a stand on these kinds of issues anymore. We will simply ride the tide and compromise. Isaiah said, "He feedeth on ashes: a deceived heart hath turned him aside, that he cannot deliver his soul, nor say, Is there not a lie in my right hand?" (Isaiah 44:20).

How much better, to provide the elderly and the shut-ins with a simple monitor, tape machine, and taped recordings of church services and other edifying programs, including tapes of well-known evangelists.

Child Sacrifice

"Moreover thou hast taken thy sons and thy daughters, whom thou hast borne unto me, and these hast thou sacrificed unto them to be devoured" (Ezekiel 16:20).

Molech was the brazen god set up in the valley of the son of Hinnom, to which idolatrous Israelites sacrificed their first-born children. It had a furnace in its belly; and when heated white hot, its extended arms served as a sacrificial altar on which babies were consumed. Jeremiah said, "They caused their sons and daughters to pass through the fire unto Molech; which I commanded them not, neither came it into my mind, that they should do this abomination, to cause Judah to sin" (Jeremiah 32:35).

Television demands child sacrifices. It is the mouth of hell, swallowing multitudes of our precious children. We permit a consuming idol to babysit them. The prophet Habakkuk called such idols "teachers of lies" (Habakkuk 2:18).

Even the cartoons now feature demons and grotesque creatures from the underworld. God's power is belittled by the superhuman powers of possessed men. I was shocked when one of my grandsons asked his mother, in all sincerity, "Mommy, who has more power, superman or Jesus?" That was before the idol was removed from their home.

I look about this nation and see a young generation so corrupt, it is almost beyond healing. I hear the heart-sob of the prophet Isaiah, speaking for the Lord, "I have nourished and brought up children, and they have rebelled against me. Ah sinful nation, a people laden with iniquity, a seed of evildoers, children that are corrupters" (Isaiah 1:2,4). "But my people know not, my people doth not consider" (Isaiah 1:3).

We are too blind to admit we've turned our own children into corrupters, those who go about spoiling, contaminating, and tearing down what is good. The prophet's lament was, "God's people don't take it to heart."

Go ahead, Mother, Dad, let the idol Baal babysit your little children. But I can promise you they will grow up, outside of a miracle, corrupted. You have allowed their minds and spirits to be stained with the indelible ink of iniquity. No one can ever stay clean after sitting under a constant barrage of that which is intrinsically evil. The continual viewing of television forges a chain of habit almost impossible to break. "If the foundations be destroyed, what can the righteous do?" (Psalm 11:3).

The headlines in a recent paper read, "House burns while family **stays glued to TV**." The whole family was so addicted, no one would leave to call the fire department.

By the time a teenager is 18, he has watched an equivalent of 6 years of television and had only 4 months of church. And people tell me it's not an idol.

One of the great passages in all of Scripture is this, "...and the children crying in the temple, Hosanna to the son of David" (Matthew 21:15). The children knew and loved Jesus. What a sight, a multitude of children moving through that staid old temple corrupted by adult money changers and thieves, hands raised, cherub-like smiles on every little face, crying at the top of their voices, "Glory to Him! Hosanna! He is the Lord!"

Isaiah prophesied of Christ, "Butter and honey shall

he eat, until he knoweth to refuse the evil and to choose the good" (Isaiah 7:15).

In contrast, how sad to see our Christian children prostrate on the floor in front of this hideous idol, eating and drinking in that which blinds them to the good and glorifies the bad. We are raising spiritual cripples, warping tender minds, and sitting idly by as they drift into moral blindness. I can see no other reason for Christ's prophecy that "Children shall rise up against their parents, and shall cause them to be put to death" (Mark 13:12), other than our having turned them into monsters with no tenderness or compassion. Television is doing just that—monsterizing innocent children.

On His way to the Cross, Jesus turned to the great company of wailing women who followed Him and said, "Daughters of Jerusalem, weep not for me, but weep for yourselves, and for your children" (Luke 23:28).

We need not weep only over godless nations; we need not weep just for future generations; we should be weeping over our own children, right now. We should be removing them far away from the idols of this age. There is enough hell for them to face outside the home. The home should be a holy, sanctified sanctuary, a place of rest and peace from the corruption of the age—and a place where Jesus is real and the Holy Spirit ever present.

My mandate from the Lord was simply to blow the trumpet and warn Christian parents that He will not hold them innocent for the destruction of their children through the idol of television.

I am not interested in Christian parents telling me they have taken this idol out of their homes. I will rejoice for them, but I will not "glory in their flesh" (Galatians 6:13,14).

We Have Forsaken the Fountain Of Living Water to Drink From Filthy Cisterns

"For my people have committed two evils; they have forsaken me the fountain of living waters, and hewed them out cisterns, broken cisterns, that can hold no water" (Jeremiah 2:13).

How appropriate that in the very next verse Jeremiah asks, "Are God's people slaves now? Why are they spoiled?" (Jeremiah 2:14).

Can such a thing be possible, that God's chosen could actually turn away, forsake the refreshing fountain of living water to sip muddy water from a polluted, diseased well? The water Jesus offered the woman at the well, water that forever satisfies thirst—rejected for a drink from a germ-laden, shallow well?

Would you call a man a fool who walks past a pure artesian well to stoop down and drink from a muddy puddle? Yet, what are Christians doing but that, when they drink in the filth of television! Is the pure water flowing in your secret closet not good enough? Must you shut off the flow of that loving well springing up in you, so you can drink of the filthy cistern you have dug for yourself? How much time do we spend now watching television, compared to the time praying for our families and for a lost world? In such an hour of impending judgment, can we spare any time in such foolishness?

Christ looks out upon the nation on a Sunday night, with millions of Christians comfortably seated in front of their television sets, drinking filthy water, and He certainly must grieve. What can Christ, our Intercessor, say to the Father but, "My people have forsaken me, the fountain of living water. They prefer cisterns."

We are developing an appetite for dirty water. We

don't want to admit how terribly it has diseased our bodies, souls, minds, and spirits. Hardly a handful will come to the living fountain on Sunday nights now! Churches, including Baptists and Pentecostals, are having to shut down the house of God on Sabbath evening. The saints are home feeding their eternal souls on filth incubated in hell. To attract a few, a movie or a musical is offered, but the church can no longer compete with television. Where is the congregation? Home—drinking in that which makes heaven weep. And incredibly, they can't seem to get enough of that tainted water; they go back for more and drink it to the full. Will God permit it, or will we be judged for it?

Think of what God is saying to us. "I am not enough for my people any more! I no longer meet their thirst, nor do I satisfy them now. They have rejected Me as their source; they thirst for another water! They have turned to the lusts of the flesh and the eye and no longer yearn after Me!"

At the last day of Feast, Jesus stood and cried, "If any man thirst, let him come unto me, and drink" (John 7:37). He told His disciples, "My blood is drink indeed." Then we hear Paul's ominous warning, "Ye cannot drink the cup of the Lord, and the cup of devils: ye cannot be partakers of the Lord's table, and of the table of devils" (1 Corinthians 10:21).

Paul asks, "Do we provoke the Lord to jealousy?" (1 Corinthians 10:22). Paul was referring to "fellowship with idols" and the drinking from the cup of the devil. Where is a true lover of Jesus who would not lay down, nay, smash any cup that provoked his Beloved to jealousy?

I know now, looking back, that my heavenly Father was very jealous of the time I robbed from Him and gave so freely to my idol. Many nights I provoked His jealousy because He waited patiently for me to come into His presence and share blessed communion, and I pushed that tug aside and planted myself before my idol and sacrificed my time to it. How many other men of God are there, parked lazily before this idol, eating junk food, getting fat and spiritually dull? How many dads spend the entire weekend gorging on sports, snacks—and neglecting wives, children, and God?

Jeremiah delivered a stinging rebuke to pastors who flirted with such idols. "The priests said not, Where is the Lord? and they that handle the law knew me not: the pastors also transgressed against me, and the prophets prophesied by Baal, and walked after things [idols] that do not profit " (Jeremiah 2:8).

The pastors were not lamenting the dearth and iniquity in God's house. They were not hungering or thirsting for a return of God's glory or for a restoration of holiness unto the Lord. None were saying, Where is God? Where is the evidence of His presence, His power, His working?

The pastors were sinning before their idols just like the people of Israel. They went about preaching without a message from God and were backslidden in heart. Their cry was not, "Thus saith the Lord!" It was a dead word from an empty vessel. Men of God who are glued to their television set end up dry and empty— and their prayer life is nearly destroyed. The result is spiritual death in both pulpit and pew.

Jeremiah said, "My people have changed their glory for that which doth not profit." The anointing, exchanged for an idol. "Yet thou sayest, Because I am innocent, surely his anger shall turn from me. Behold, I will plead with thee, because thou sayest, I have not sinned" (Jeremiah 2:35).

Ministers can waste hours viewing visions of hell and saying to God, "I am innocent. I have not sinned." I know, I've said that to myself and to God for years.

"Nothing sinful about it—no harm—God isn't angry—just relaxation—a change of pace." Spending hours watching sports, another idol for many, and robbing God of that precious time leads to loss of vision and glory. No wonder so many of our churches are twice dead and plucked up by the roots.

We are just like the children of Israel, stubborn and self-willed and determined to indulge in the sins of the heathen. Jeremiah wrote, "Behold, I will lay stumblingblocks before this people, and the fathers and the sons together shall fall upon them" (Jeremiah 6:21). We have been deceived by Satan into thinking television is simply a diversion rather than an abomination.

One of the greatest curses of this idol has been the loss of urgency about the return of Christ and impending judgment. We've laughed so hard with Lucy, we can't make ourselves get very serious about going home to glory. We are laughing when we ought to be laying before God with a broken heart and a contrite spirit. We are laughing ourselves right out of an awareness of soon-coming judgment.

It is almost impossible today to arouse a crowd of Christians about the nearness of Christ's coming. Even the warnings of the final wrath of God is greeted with a big "ho-hum." We have been sedated by all the visions of terror, violence, turmoil, and tragedy we've seen so much of on television. The end of the world, the judgments of God on sinful man—it's just another horror picture. Nothing seems real anymore because television has turned life into one great fantasy celluloid reel.

God needs some fearless prophets to bring us back to reality. Life is not just another television series, and the impending judgment on the nation is very real.

What About Balance?

I hear it everywhere I go: "Television has a knob on it; we can always turn it off. We need to keep our balance on these things and not get fanatical." Hear me good! Balance is a code word for a divided heart. It is used by lukewarm Christians to hold on to all kinds of idols. And who is turning off the knob? Who is watching only "the good stuff"?

I think God has come to hate the word balance—because what He is seeking now is radical Christianity. With a nuclear holocaust hanging heavy over this nation, what should we be but radical in our service and devotion! God is calling for Holy Ghost radicals who will cast down all idols, come to His holy hill with clean hands and pure hearts, and live detached from this world, having in them an eternal vision. God wants to smash all idols.

The Belly God and Others

Down with the belly god! Down with the idol of food! Down with gluttony and surfeiting! Down with the gorging, the lusting for food, the addiction to delicacies—while the world teeters on the brink of destruction. Christians are not much aware of their worshipping the food god. We are becoming an obese people, more fond of eating and drinking than purification and preparing. Shame on us! Balance? Forget it! We must get radical and deal with these idols unmercifully while there is still time.

Down with the information idol! No time for God's Word, but all the time needed to flood the mind with information. Magazines, books, computers, periodicals—we feel the need to stay informed. But it has become an idol to multitudes, including ministers. Pull it down—get back to revelation, back to the cleansing, healing Word of God.

Away with substituting one idol for another. I see Christians tearing down their television idol only to replace it with food, movies, sports, recreation, foolish magazines, and worthless books. One of the reasons God wants the television out is to make time for prayer, Bible study, and spiritual growth. If the time saved is not invested wisely, you will substitute another idol. Keep your television if you are not committed to filling the time saved with prayer and seeking God. Discipline yourself—bring your thoughts under subjection to the Lord Jesus. Stay in His Word until it becomes a new Book to you—until you are drawn to it, until it works its sweet cleansing power in you. Those who draw near to Him don't need television anymore. "What have I to do any more with idols? I have heard him, and observed him" (Hosea 14:8).

Television Evangelists

What about the television evangelists who need the support of Christians to stay on? Missionaries are supported all over the world, and you never see them on television. You are seldom in touch with them; yet, you give because you have a heart for the gospel. Also, we have been led to believe that television is being used to evangelize the lost. If so, why do I need one in my home?

Jeremiah said, "Shall a man make gods unto himself, and they are no gods?" (Jeremiah 16:20). Satan does not own the airwaves, even though he corrupts them. Television becomes a god of this world only as it is animated by the spirit of Satan. Otherwise, it is but an electronic marvel, a piece of furniture.

It is possible for an anointed pastor or evangelist to use television to reach the lost for Christ. Multitudes have been saved watching a telecast. When anointed by the gospel, television can become a powerful tool of evangelism. They are not in collusion with an idol—they are using the medium to the glory of God. It is idolatrous only because of that which animates it at any given time.

The few evangelists who are worth listening to are those who preach repentance and who show the nation its sins. Those who use television as an offering basket and a showcase for their expensive projects have misused it and ought not to be supported by any Christ-loving believer. Those who call the nation to repentance deserve our support. But few they are, indeed. I suggest believers send all their support only to those preaching repentance. I have a few television evangelist friends I intend to support wholeheartedly.

I prefer not to have television in my home because I do not need to be evangelized, I can support the few I trust without seeing their programs, and because every time the "on" button is pushed, it has horrifying potential for demonic influence and activity. I do not want to be of the naive majority of Christians who claim their "maturity" permits them to watch any kind of program without being adversely affected. That just is not so. The truly mature will tremble at God's Word, see it for its potential danger, and shun it completely.

One man's opinion? Say that if you will, but along with a host of other believers who have heard the same word from heaven, we are enjoying the freedom and release from an idol that once held us in terrible bondage—and it is glorious! I will not judge my brother or sister who disagrees with this message, and I want nothing to do with legalistic demands that "It must go—or else!" Let every believer seek the Lord for conviction and direction. Do nothing until led by the Spirit of God.

"I Am Not Convicted"

That is what so many Christians tell me, and I say that can be a cop-out. I prayed about it, and here is what I believe. Once the Word is clearly revealed on the subject, it is not a matter any longer of being convicted—it is simply a matter of obedience.

I am going to give you thirty-one scriptural reasons for ridding your home of this idol. If one chooses to be carnal or lukewarm, these verses have no claim. But for those who yearn to be in the bride of Christ, they will be priceless. They are clear, powerful, and to the point. Once you hear the Word of the Lord, it will come down only to obedience or disobedience.

Thirty-One Scriptural Reasons Why Overcoming Christians Should Remove the Idol Of Television From Their Homes

"To this man will I look, even to him that is poor and of a contrite spirit, and trembleth at my word" (Isaiah 66:2).

1. We have a direct commandment not to bring it into our homes.

"Neither shalt thou bring an abomination into thine house, lest thou be a cursed thing like it: but thou shalt utterly detest it, and thou shalt utterly abhor it; for it is a cursed thing" (Deuteronomy 7:26).

2. It puts viewers in the seat of the scornful.

"Blessed is the man that walketh not in the counsel of the ungodly, nor standeth in the way of sinners, nor sitteth in the seat of the scornful. But his delight is in the law of the Lord; and in his law doth he meditate day and night. And he shall be like a tree planted by the rivers of water, that bringeth forth his fruit in his season; his leaf also shall not wither; and whatsoever he doeth shall prosper" (Psalm 1:1-3).

3. Overcomers are not to set any wicked thing before their eyes.

"I will behave myself wisely in a perfect way. O when wilt thou come unto me? I will walk within my house with a perfect heart. I will set no wicked thing before ' mine eyes: I hate the work of them that turn aside; it shall not cleave to me" (Psalm 101:2,3).

4. When animated by Satan it is fellowshipping with the works of darkness.

"Be ye not unequally yoked together with unbelievers: for what fellowship hath righteousness with unrighteousness? and what communion hath light with darkness?" (2 Corinthians 6:14).

5. It pollutes the pure stream of righteous thoughts.

"Finally, brethren, whatsoever things are true, whatsoever things are honest, whatsoever things are just, whatsoever things are pure, whatsoever things are lovely, whatsoever things are of good report; if there be any virtue, and if there be any praise, think on these things" (Philippians 4:8).

6. It is touching the unclean thing that Paul warned against.

"And what agreement hath the temple of God with idols? for ye are the temple of the living God; as God hath said, I will dwell in them, and walk in them; and I will be their God, and they shall be my people. Wherefore come out from among them, and be ye separate, saith the Lord, and touch not the unclean thing; and I will receive you" (2 Corinthians 6:16,17).

7. It is unsuited to the bride preparing herself for Christ.

"And I John saw the holy city, new Jerusalem, coming down from God out of heaven, prepared as a bride adorned for her husband" (Revelation 21:2).

"...to make ready a people prepared for the Lord" (Luke 1:17).

8. We are not to waste time, but redeem it.

"Wherefore he saith, Awake thou that sleepest, and arise from the dead, and Christ shall give thee light. See then that ye walk circumspectly, not as fools, but as wise, redeeming the time, because the days are evil" (Ephesians 5:14-16).

9. We are not to partake with idols of the children of disobedience.

"But fornication, and all uncleanness, or covetousness, let it not be once named among you, as becometh saints; neither filthiness, nor foolish talking, nor jesting, which are not convenient: but rather giving of thanks. For this ye know, that no whoremonger, nor unclean person, nor covetous man, who is an idolater, hath any inheritance in the kingdom of Christ and of God. Let no man deceive you with vain words: for because of these things cometh the wrath of God upon the children of disobedience. Be not ye therefore partakers with them. For ye were sometimes darkness, but now are ye light in the Lord: walk as children of light: (for the fruit of the Spirit is in all goodness and righteousness and truth;) proving what is acceptable unto the Lord. And have no fellowship with the unfruitful works of darkness, but rather reprove them. For it is a shame even to speak of those things which are done of them in secret. But all things that are reproved are made manifest by the light: for whatsoever doth make manifest is light" (Ephesians 5:3-13).

10. Viewers are in the seat of violence which takes away grief for sin.

"Woe to them that are at ease in Zion...that put far away the evil day, and cause the seat of violence to come near; that lie upon beds of ivory...but they are not grieved for the affliction of Joseph" (Amos 6:1,3,4,6).

11. It certainly does not renew the mind.

"I beseech you therefore, brethren, by the mercies of God, that ye present your bodies a living sacrifice, holy, acceptable unto God, which is your reasonable service. And be not conformed to this world: but be ye transformed by the renewing of your mind, that ye may prove what is that good, and acceptable, and perfect, will of God" (Romans 12:1,2).

12. It represents the leaven of the world and should be purged from the home.

"Your glorying is not good. Know ye not that a little leaven leaveneth the whole lump? Purge out therefore the old leaven, that ye may be a new lump, as ye are unleavened. For even Christ our passover is sacrificed for us" (1 Corinthians 5:6,7).

13. We are to mortify all that is unclean and idolatrous.

"If ye then be risen with Christ, seek those things which are above, where Christ sitteth on the right hand of God. Set your affection on things above, not on things on the earth. For ye are dead, and your life is hid with Christ in God. Mortify therefore your members which are upon the earth; fornication, uncleanness, inordinate affection, evil concupiscence, and covetousness, which is idolatry: for which things' sake the wrath of God cometh on the children of disobedience" (Colossians 3:1,2,3,5,6).

14. It is a filthy communication that we are commanded to put off.

"But now ye also put off all these; anger, wrath, malice, blasphemy, filthy communication out of your mouth" (Colossians 3:8).

15. It is not walking worthy of God, unblameable and holy.

"Ye are witnesses, and God also, how holily and justly and unblameably we behaved ourselves among you that believe: as ye know how we exhorted and comforted and charged every one of you, as a father doth his children, that ye would walk worthy of God, who hath called you unto his kingdom and glory" (1 Thessalonians 2:10-12).

16. Viewers are not possessing their vessel in sanctification and honor.

"For this is the will of God, even your sanctification, that ye should abstain from fornication: that every one of you should know how to possess his vessel in sanctification and honour; for God hath not called us unto uncleanness, but unto holiness" (1 Thessalonians 4:3,4,7).

17. It is a polluted fountain out of which proceeds cursing and bitterness.

"Out of the same mouth proceedeth blessing and cursing. My brethren, these things ought not so to be. Doth a fountain send forth at the same place sweet water and bitter? Can the fig tree, my brethren, bear olive berries? either a vine, figs? So can no fountain both yield salt water and fresh" (James 3:10-12).

18. It takes away the blush toward sin.

"Were they ashamed when they had committed abomination? Nay, they were not at all ashamed, neither could they blush: therefore shall they fall among them that fall: in the time of their visitation they shall be cast down, saith the Lord" (Jeremiah 8:12).

19. Christ calls us to anoint our eyes, not poison them.

"And anoint thine eyes with eyesalve, that thou mayest see" (Revelation 3:18).

20. We are to cleanse ourselves from all filthiness of the flesh, perfecting holiness in the fear of God.

"Having therefore these promises, dearly beloved, let us cleanse ourselves from all filthiness of the flesh and spirit, perfecting holiness in the fear of God" (2 Corinthians 7:1).

21. A ministry to Christ demands we renounce hidden things of dishonesty.

"Therefore seeing we have this ministry, as we have received mercy, we faint not; but have renounced the hidden things of dishonesty, not walking in craftiness, nor handling the word of God deceitfully; but by manifestation of the truth commending ourselves to every man's conscience in the sight of God" (2 Corinthians 4:1,2).

22. It is an idol that causes confusion and should be hated.

"Confounded be all they that serve graven images, that boast themselves of idols: worship him, all ye gods. Ye that love the Lord, hate evil: he preserveth the souls of his saints; he delivereth them out of the hand of the wicked" (Psalm 97:7,10).

23. It offends children, causing them to stumble.

"And whosoever shall offend one of these little ones that believe in me, it is better for him that a millstone were hanged about his neck, and he were cast into the sea" (Mark 9:42).

24. Viewing becomes a dominating sin of presumption.

"The law of the Lord is perfect, converting the soul: the testimony of the Lord is sure, making wise the simple. The statutes of the Lord are right, rejoicing the heart: the commandment of the Lord is pure, enlightening the eyes. The fear of the Lord is clean, enduring for ever: the judgments of the Lord are true and righteous altogether. More to be desired are they than gold, yea, than much fine gold: sweeter also than honey and the honeycomb. Moreover by them is thy servant warned: and in keeping of them there is great reward. Who can understand his errors? cleanse thou me from secret faults. Keep back thy servant also from presumptuous sins; let them not have dominion over me: then shall I be upright, and I shall be innocent from the great transgression. Let the words of my mouth, and the meditation of my heart, be acceptable in thy sight, O Lord, my strength, and my redeemer" (Psalm 19:7-14).

25. It is too late. Christ is coming soon. We should be casting off all works of darkness.

"The night is far spent, the day is at hand: let us therefore cast off the works of darkness, and let us put on the armour of light. Let us walk honestly, as in the day; not in rioting and drunkenness, not in chambering and wantonness, not in strife and envying. But put ye on the Lord Jesus Christ, and make not provision for the flesh, to fulfill the lusts thereof" (Romans 13:12-14).

"And every man that hath this hope in him purifieth himself, even as he is pure" (1 John 3:3).

26. God commands holy people to destroy and cut down all idols.

"But thus shall ye deal with them; ye shall destroy their altars, and break down their images, and cut down their groves, and burn their graven images with fire. For thou art an holy people unto the Lord thy God: the Lord thy God hath chosen thee to be a special people unto himself, above all people that are upon the face of the earth" (Deuteronomy 7:5,6).

27. It is friendship with the world, causing enmity with God.

"Ye ask, and receive not, because ye ask amiss, that ye may consume it upon your lusts. Ye adulterers and adulteresses, know ye not that the friendship of the world is enmity with God? whosoever therefore will be a friend of the world is the enemy of God" (James 4:3,4).

28. The face of the Lord is against them that do evil, and viewers are not eschewing evil as commanded.

"For he that will love life, and see good days, let him refrain his tongue from evil, and his lips that they speak no guile: let him eschew evil, and do good; let him seek peace, and ensue it. For the eyes of the Lord are over the righteous, and his ears are open unto their prayers: but the face of the Lord is against them that do evil. And who is he that will harm you, if ye be followers of that which is good?" (1 Peter 3:10-13).

29. If you consider it only a spot on your garment, it is still wrong.

"Wherefore, beloved, seeing that ye look for such things, be diligent that ye may be found of him in peace, without spot, and blameless" (2 Peter 3:14).

"Ye therefore, beloved, seeing ye know these things before, beware lest ye also, being led away with the error of the wicked, fall from your own stedfastness" (2 Peter 3:17).

30. Television encompasses all three temptations Satan introduced in Eden.

"Love not the world, neither the things that are in the world. If any man love the world, the love of the Father is not in him. For all that is in the world, the lust of the flesh, and the lust of the eyes, and the pride of life, is not of the Father, but is of the world. And the world passeth away, and the lust thereof: but he that doeth the will of God abideth for ever" (1 John 2:15-17).

31. **Overcomers who have seen the Lord in His glory don't need it!**

"What have I to do any more with idols? I have heard him, and observed him" (Hosea 14:8).

Conclusion

Shall we tremble at His Word and obey—or shall we make excuses and continue sitting in the seat of the scornful? Will we become so enthralled with Christ that we can no longer gaze upon that which would grieve Him?

Will the bride of Christ truly separate from all that is of this world? Are there any in this nation who can hear and accept this message? Or, are we too sedated by the addictions of this world to hear?

Will the church of Jesus Christ call me a legalist, a self-proclaimed judge? Or, will the Spirit raise up an anointed body of saints to shake off all entanglements and cry out for cleansing and separation?

We shall see!

Chapter 4
The Music of Devils
In God's House

"But they set their abominations in the house, which is called by my name, to defile it" (Jeremiah 32:34).

I was shocked beyond measure recently when I opened a Christian magazine and saw the picture of a "heavy metal" rock group calling themselves Christians. They were dressed in the very same sadomasochist costumes I had seen while witnessing for Christ on the streets of San Francisco.

I conjured in my mind all kinds of evil visions. I remember well how I felt on the streets of that city as ten to twelve sadomasochists came walking toward me, dressed in black leather with nail-studded belts and bracelets, chains, metal collars, punk hair-dos, and painted faces. Their eyes were wild, and their expressions, forlorn and spacey. They approached me like rebellious demons on the prowl, daring me to stay on the sidewalk. I stepped aside to let them pass, but I knew I had just seen the devil in men, walking.

I cannot explain to you the horror in my soul when I saw the picture of the "Christian heavy metal" group—claiming to be ambassadors of Christ—dressed in the very same costumes, with the very same hair styles, the very same threatening expressions, playing the same kind of music the sadomasochists dance to. Zephaniah predicted, "It shall come to pass in the day of the Lord's sacrifice, that I will punish the princes, and the king's children, and all such as are clothed with strange apparel" (Zephaniah 1:8). Paul said of them, "For such are false apostles, deceitful workers, transforming themselves into the apostles of Christ. And no marvel; for Satan himself is transformed into an angel of light. Therefore, it is no great thing if his ministers also be transformed as the ministers of righteousness; whose end shall be according to their works" (2 Corinthians 11:13-15). Jesus said of these kind: "For there shall arise false Christs, and false prophets, and shall shew great signs and wonders; insomuch that, if it were possible, they shall deceive the very elect. Behold, I have told you before" (Matthew 24:24,25).

I heard the inner groaning of my spirit crying out, "How low we have fallen! Punk rock in the holy place? God forbid! My dear Lord, look at what seeks passage through the rent veil, all in the name of Christ!" With Jeremiah, God's true people say, "We are confounded, because we have heard reproach: shame hath covered our faces: for strangers are come into the sanctuaries of the Lord's house" (Jeremiah 51:51).

Where is the alarm in Zion, where is the shame, where are the prophets who should be crying aloud, "Enough! No more music of devils in the house of God"? I hear the booming voice of the prophet Isaiah crying out, "...the Lord will take away the bravery of their anklets about their feet, and their fancy lace, the chains, the bracelets, the ornaments of the legs, the head bands, the earrings, and nose jewels....It shall be a stink" (Isaiah 3:18-24).

Is this the overcoming church, pure and spotless and separated from the world—where such horrible wickedness is welcomed, as long as it is disguised in the sheep clothes of religion? Is God's house now a place where even demonic expressions find a place with music borrowed from the altars of Baal? We are seeing Christ being wounded by those who claim to know Him. "And one shall say unto him, What are these wounds in thine hands? Then he shall answer, Those with which I was wounded in the house of my friends" (Zechariah 13:6).

What kind of cowardly ministry do we have in the land now that will tolerate and even applaud music that makes angels blush? Why aren't we denouncing these false prophets of music who are deceiving so many? Jesus said, "Take heed that no man deceive you. For many shall come in my name, saying, I am Christ; and shall deceive many" (Matthew 24:4,5). They will testify they are of Christ, but the gospel they preach is another gospel and theirs is another Jesus. "I marvel that ye are so soon removed from him that called you into the grace of Christ unto another gospel: which is not another; but there be some that trouble you, and would pervert the gospel of Christ" (Galatians 1:6,7).

The ungodly music creeping into God's house today has to be the wonder of heaven, the disbelief of all that is celestial, the grief of the four and twenty elders around God's holy throne. The question in glory has to be, how can those who call themselves by Christ's holy name take coals off Satan's personal altars and bring them into God's presence, to lay them on His altar? The angels must be asking, "Are they so blind? Don't they know they are offering strange fire with strange coals? There is hell fire in each coal! There is damnation in it! Priests of God have been killed for such abomination! Don't they know God will destroy those who enter the holy place with strange fire? How can this be?" "But they set their abominations in the temple, which is called by my name, to defile it" (Jeremiah 32:34).

Desecraters of the Holy Altar

Who are these "heavy metal" and "punk rock" groups who claim they have come in the name of Jesus? Who are the rockers and the innovators in God's house? They are desecraters of God's holy altar! There is a fearful picture of them in the Old Testament that should put the fear of God in them and all who cater to them.

They are represented by Ahaz, a compromising king of Israel who was corrupted by his friendship with heathen. Let every Christian, who fears the Lord and who grieves over the sacrilegious innovations in God's house, study the sixteenth chapter of Second Kings. It describes perfectly what we are seeing today in the way of desecration of holy things.

King Ahaz did that which was evil in the eyes of the Lord. His great weakness corrupted him; he was a friend of the wicked King Tigleth-pileser of Assyria. By his own admission, he was "servant and son" to this heathen power. He was as much at home in the heathen temples of Damascus as in the Lord's house in Jerusalem, having never separated himself exclusively for God. His heart was charmed by what he saw in the heathen temples of Assyria. "And he saw an altar that was in Damascus: and King Ahaz sent to Urijah the priest the fashion of the altar, and the pattern of it, according to all the workmanship thereof. And Urijah the priest built an altar according to all that King Ahaz had sent from Damascus" (2 Kings 16:10,11).

What is this? A new, innovative altar, one copied from the heathen gods of Assyria, being erected in God's house? And the priests not only did not denounce it, but went along with it. This sniveling priest "did according to all King Ahaz commanded." What a picture of the compromising ministers of this day who fall right in line with heathen innovations in God's house. They have no backbone; they are afraid to denounce the very changes and innovations that desecrate the Lord's altar. So it is today—ministers and churches go right along with the music desecration. The cry is, "Don't judge," and that is Satan's smokescreen to hide all kinds of evil ways.

Outrageous! A corrupt king—chained and charmed by heathen altars, in cooperation with a spineless priesthood—set up a new altar, right in front of God's holy altar. This new altar was a perfect replica of those upon which the heathen sacrificed to their deities. Isn't that what rock music is among believers—a replica of that which is served up on the altars of Satan at wild and heathenish concerts?

Insult was added to injury. King Ahaz "brought also the brasen altar, which was before the Lord, from the forefront of the house, from between the altar and the house of the Lord, and put it on the north side of the altar" (2 Kings 16:14). He rearranged God's house, putting God's altar in the background and his altar in the forefront. Then upon his heathen replica altar he blasphemed by offering sacrifices. The blood of Christ, represented by the sacrifices, was profaned. The blood-red stripes of Jesus Christ were made a mockery before all the house of Israel and the heathen world. Incredibly, the priests permitted it, were involved in the conspiracy, and no one raised a voice against the profaneness of it all.

It was inevitable that King Ahaz would desecrate the laver and the brazen sea. Holy standards had to be brought down. The laver represents cleansing, purity, holiness. But King Ahaz "cut off the borders of the bases, and removed the laver from off them; and took down the sea from off the brasen oxen that were under it, and put it upon the pavement of stones" (2 Kings 16:17).

Read and tremble, saints of God. With the ministry giving silent assent, this innovator, this desecrater of God's altar took the laver off its pedestal and laid it on the pavement. It was an outright act of devaluing righteousness, bringing holiness down to the dirt, making cleansing unimportant. Purity was brought down to street level. It was put down and put aside—neglected. This is what these new music innovators are doing: devaluing holiness and making a mockery of purity and separation from the world.

Ahaz proclaimed for himself a special anointing to sacrifice to Jehovah on his innovative new altar. It was the most absurd worship possible: blood sacrifices to Jehovah God, on a newly created heathen altar, by a man who thought he was right. Heathenism had woven a complete spell over him, until he was totally blind to all true spiritual values. He thought he was worshipping God on his self-made altar, while all the while God was infuriated by the abomination of it all. That is the story of the rock lovers. They are introducing heathen ways of worship—false worship. They think they are worshipping the Lord, while all the while He despises their offerings. They use the name of Jesus to justify their heathen practices.

Borrowed rock music is Satan's calculated attempt to pollute the worship of almighty God. It is worship that he is after; it is worship he so desires for himself. Satan will go to any extreme to pollute the worship directed to the Lord so that it will be rejected. In this way he succeeds in hindering worship in spirit and in truth. He simply adds another spirit and mixes in a lie, knowing God will reject it. God must, and always does, reject all worship that is not born of the Holy Spirit and that is not all of truth. And even if that music inspires the performers and listeners, it does not get beyond the ceiling—God won't touch it. He abhors it!

Ahaz ended up "shutting the doors of the house of the Lord" (2 Chronicles 28:24). He took his novelty altar to all the high places where the gods of their wicked world had been erected. God's house is too restrictive, too holy for these kind, so they take their novelty Jesus acts into bars, clubs, and other satanic turfs. They think the older believers are out of touch.

Every priest, every Israelite who worshipped at that mock altar was guilty of blaspheming, along with Ahaz, the perpetrater. And I say that any TV station, radio station, pastor, young person calling themselves Christian, who give even silent assent to these pagan innovations, will be held accountable to God.

"But they sound so sincere. They really do love Jesus. They take Christ where few others can. They're not bad; just different." It could be said of King Ahaz that he was sincere but very wrong, perverted in his knowledge of Jehovah and set up a corrupted way of worship. It is still black and ugly abomination in God's eyes. So should it be in ours. We are to go into the world to win sinners—but not to copy their ways. There must be no compromise in this area of lifestyle.

May God give us more preachers with enough zeal for His holiness to denounce these innovators and drive them out of God's house, back to where they belong—with their heathen friends—to perform before the altars of demons. We should pray for them first; some may be saved from deception. If they will not hear God's convicting Word and will not repent and turn from their wicked ways, we should do what Paul commanded and reject them as heretics and "not so much as to eat with them" (Titus 3:10).

Most incredible of all, "They feared the Lord, and

served their own gods" (2 Kings 17:33). And, "unto this day they do after their former manners" (2 Kings 17:34).

Thank God for King Hezekiah, the son of Ahaz. He swept away the phony altars of his father and cleaved to the Lord and "he rebelled against the King of Assyria, and served him not" (2 Kings 18:7). There finally came a man of God with a holy backbone.

Rock Addiction

It amazes me that such a great multitude of young men and women, including young ministers, are so infatuated with rock music. They've been raised on it. In every other area of their life, the Lord is in full control. They are dedicated, pure in every other way—but they cling to this one idol. Just one thing stands between them and God's very best. They'll give up TV, sports, illicit sex, overeating, and all other kinds of idols—but don't dare trod their music. How true, "a scorner heareth not rebuke" (Proverbs 13:1).

I cringe when I hear parents and ministers say, "Don't judge." I say they had better obey God's Word and judge righteous judgment, before they lose their children to the seductions of this age. Jesus judged the Pharisees, calling them vipers. Paul judged Peter for being "carried away" by error.

Parents are now so easy and nonchalant about the music their kids listen to. They say, "Well, each generation has its own style of music. We don't like it, but it seems the kids like it. And they do sing about Jesus, so it must be all right." What incredible spiritual blindness!

We have come to the place where anything is acceptable if it "gets results." If the music of devils gets kids up front to make a decision, it is acceptable. How very dangerous. Most of those youth have not been touched beyond their emotions. The Holy Spirit has not probed deeply to deal with sin. No demands have been made on them about forsaking the world, their old ways and friends—and there is little or no heart repentance. It ends up a vote for Jesus. God in His infinite mercy brings some of them through, but only because of other works of conviction in them.

One of the reasons God's Spirit was lifted from the Jesus Movement of the last decade was their refusal to forsake their old music. They gave up pot, heroin, alcohol, promiscuous sex, and they even gave up perverted lifestyles. But they refused to give up their beloved rock. "But now, after that ye have known God, or rather are known of God, how turn ye again to the weak and beggarly elements, whereunto ye desire again to be in bondage?" (Galatians 4:9). Like Israel, they "brought up" their whoredoms from Egypt. "Neither left she her whoredoms brought from Egypt: for in her youth they lay with her, and they bruised the breasts of her virginity, and poured their whoredom upon her. Wherefore I have delivered her into the hand of her lovers" (Ezekiel 23:8,9).

Amazing! I say its hold is stronger than drugs, alcohol, or tobacco. It is the biggest mass addiction in the world's history. Will they still be holding on to it tenaciously before the judgment seat of Christ? Will Christ say, "I told you one thing was lacking; one idol remained. You went your stubborn way—you let your life be ruled by a music that grieved me, all because you would not give Me everything!" "But thou hast made me to serve with thy sins, thou hast wearied me with thine iniquities" (Isaiah 43:24).

What Is Rock

What is rock? How can you distinguish it in these days of drums, electric guitars, heavy bass, and complicated rhythms? I cannot answer that in any technical way. Since it is primarily a soul and spirit matter, it can't be judged only on technicalities. All I know is that the Spirit of God within me knows, and He lets me feel His grief over it. Those who adore Christ and who worship Him in Spirit and truth will learn to discern it quickly. A good test is to spend a few hours in the closet of prayer in the presence of Jesus. Let the Spirit of God melt your heart and crumble your pride. Open your heart there to the deep probings of the Spirit, and ask Him to show you what is right and what is wrong. Be truly open to the mind of God. Spend another hour studying the Word of God. While in the Spirit of deep worship turn on your music! You will know within seconds. "And thine ears shall hear a word behind thee, saying, This is the way, walk ye in it, when ye turn to the right hand, and when ye turn to the left" (Isaiah 30:21). Deep calls to deep, and the Spirit of God in you will resist all that comes out of the womb of Satan. There can be no legalistic rules; it is a matter of Spirit and truth.

Isaiah said you will find your song and the right music when a holy solemnity is upon you. "Ye shall have a song, as in the night when a holy solemnity is kept; and gladness of heart, as when one goeth with a pipe to come into the mountain of the Lord, to the mighty One of Israel" (Isaiah 30:29). That holy solemnity has been replaced by foolishness and joking.

There is no doubt in my mind now—rock music, as used and performed in Christian circles, is of the same satanic seed as that which is called punk, heavy metal, and is performed in devilish rock concerts worldwide.

That is the trumpet message God commanded me to send forth. Few will listen, but the bride of Christ will! They will sing, "The Lord God hath opened mine ear, and I was not rebellious, neither turned away back" (Isaiah 50:5).

Isaiah said, "This is a rebellious people, lying children, children that will not hear the law of the Lord: which say to the seers, See not; and to the prophets, Prophesy not unto us right things, speak unto us smooth things" (Isaiah 30:9-10).

God and Rock

I am not much interested in what preachers or musicians have to say about rock. My own opinion is not worth much either. I am not the judge of what is acceptable or unacceptable to the Lord in the way of music. All the books and sermons about the evils of rock music have not changed many young minds. Christian musicians still perform it; Christian youth still devour it; and it keeps spreading in the church.

My only concern is, What does God think about rock? If we can discover His mind on this matter, then all Christ-loving youth must accept it; and if they won't, it will prove they are stubborn, deceived by lying spirits, and not willing to submit to the Holy Spirit's authority.

I have prostrated myself before God, seeking His mind on this matter, because the end of all things is near; and this is not the time to be indulging in anything that God may hate, especially any kind of music. We need to leave this ruined scene singing and worshipping in Spirit and in truth. And I don't believe true overcomers want to be involved with anything Christ simply tolerates, and especially they don't want to touch anything God may detest. Arguing on the basis of some kind of legalistic standard does not work. The only question important is: Does God bless or hate rock music in His holy place? Will He permit it in His house or cast it out, like an accursed thing? Believe it or not, God's Word has the answers—putting the matter beyond all question; and it will come down to whether or not each reader is willing to put aside all preconceived ideas and simply hear God's Word. It is absolute spiritual blindness to hold on to something that may be truly despicable in God's eyes.

The Holy Spirit revealed to me four truths that I believe fully manifest His attitude about rock music and all other kinds of worldly music in His house. Those who want to face the judgment seat of Christ with holy assurance need to hear what the Spirit is saying.

Four Considerations That Reveal God's Attitude About Rock Music in His Temple

Only God-fearing, Christ-loving, devoted Christians will take the time to study and consider these biblical precepts. Those with closed minds will not even consider God's Word on the subject.

1. Out of which womb was the music born?

It is very clear in the Word that where God deals with men or issues, He goes back to the womb. God is mostly concerned with the seed that produces the fruit. All seed produces its own kind.

God reminded Israel He had carried them not just out of Egypt, but that He was their deliverer when they were still in the womb. "Hearken unto me, O house of Jacob, and all the remnant of the house of Israel, which are borne by me from the belly, which are carried from the womb" (Isaiah 46:3).

The twenty-second Psalm is the cry of our Lord Jesus from the cross. Looking up to His heavenly Father, Jesus prayed, "Thou art he that took me out of the womb: thou didst make me hope when I was upon my mother's breasts. I was cast upon thee from the womb: thou art my God from my mother's belly" (Psalm 22:9,10).

Was rock music born in the womb of a Spirit-filled musician? Was the music cast upon the Lord from the belly after birth, and could it be said that it was God's from inception? Did the Holy Spirit give it birth?

Let me remind you why God had to finally give up on the Israelites in the desert. God forsook them and let them rot away in a snake-infested wilderness because they were rebels from the womb. Even though He had carried them since conception, God said of them, "I knew that thou wouldest deal very treacherously, and wast called a transgressor from the womb" (Isaiah 48:8).

A transgressor from the womb! Does this describe rock music? Hosea the prophet said of Israel, "They have deeply corrupted themselves...and they loved their evil deeds...woe to them when I depart from them" (Hosea 9:9-12). Then he warned, "Their glory shall fly away like a bird, from the birth, and from the womb, and from the conception" (Hosea 9:11). And because of their sinful hearts, Hosea cried out, "Give them a miscarrying womb and dry breasts...they shall bear no fruit...I will slay even the beloved fruit of their womb" (Hosea 9:14-16).

Whatever is evil and wicked is divorced from God from its inception. "The wicked are estranged [alienated] from the womb: they go astray as soon as they be born, speaking lies" (Psalm 58:3). Then David added, "Their poison is like the poison of a serpent: they are like the deaf adder that stoppeth her ear; which will not hearken to the voice of charmers, charming never so wisely" (Psalm 58:4,5).

Rock music was born in the womb of darkness and rebellion. There is a new generation today that has no contact with the roots of rock; it was before their time. Had they seen how it was born, with all the drugs, dropping out, rebellion, and devil worship—they may have had a better understanding of what I mean by its "womb." When it was first born and broke on the scene years ago, every Spirit-filled lover of Christ discerned it was a transgression. Thirty years ago, when Elvis Presley made his debut, I fell on my face before God and wept. The Spirit of God in me grieved. Even some secular musicians denounced it as evil-spirited. I wrote a book shortly after entitled, Rock and Roll, The Devil's Heartbeat. That is what it was in its inception; that is what it still is, because it is the fruit of an evil seed. It is the fruit of the womb of wickedness, and it soon was exposed for what it truly was and still is: the anthem of rebellion and lawlessness. I put in the same category all music, including country western and pop—when sin is glorified and the music and words are sensual. Still there are some Christian youth who nearly worship the memory of Elvis, "King of Rock and Roll."

If you were to tell me that rock was not born of a wicked womb, then you fit perfectly the description of the Psalmist of one who is like a deaf adder who will listen to no one. You are the one who "stoppeth his ears" and will not listen. It is serpentine blindness. You are under the spell of a lying spirit.

How can anyone who adores Jesus Christ take an evil child, born of evil seed, of an evil womb, and make it a servant to Him? Jesus said, "Give to Caesar that which belongs to Caesar, and give to God what belongs to God." Jesus said, "A good tree cannot bring forth evil fruit, neither can a corrupt tree bring forth good fruit. Every tree that bringeth not forth good fruit is hewn down, and cast into the fire" (Matthew 7:18,19).

The Bible speaks much about the fruit of the womb. John the Baptist was "filled with the Holy Ghost from his mother's womb" (Luke 1:15). The womb of John's mother produced a holy prophet, a godly fruit from a godly seed. What kind of fruit does rock and roll produce? Godliness and purity? A hunger and thirst for

Christ? A broken and a contrite heart? Conviction for sin? Be honest!

According to God's Word, all seed bears "after its own kind" (Genesis 1:12). When the Beatles, the original rockers, mocked Jesus Christ and glorified drugs in their music, what kind of fruit was that? When 400,000 youth gathered at Woodstock years ago, staying high for three whole days on rock and pot, and going forth to a decade of violence, what kind of fruit was that? From its inception, rock and roll has produced nothing but evil fruit. Rock has dry breasts and can give life and health to no one.

Sadly, even though God is revealing His wrath against that which is born of Satan, there are a host who will "Come and stand before me in this house, which is called by my name, and say, We are delivered to do all these abominations? Is this house, which is called by my name, become a den of robbers in your eyes? Behold, even I have seen it, saith the Lord" (Jeremiah 7:10,11).

2. God will not accept a blemished sacrifice.

God Himself called His church a house of sacrifice (2 Chronicles 7:12). Every time a child of God preaches, prays, praises, or sings—he is bringing a sacrificial offering unto the Lord. Every Christian concert or record is an offering unto the Lord.

The sacrificial lamb the Israelites were to bring to the altar had to be "without blemish" (Exodus 12:5). They were to be without spot and could not be lame or sickly.

What has this to do with rock music in the church? How can it apply to Christians who perform or listen to it? It should be obvious. In worship or praise, our Father will not receive, but rather He will furiously reject any offering that is polluted or spotted in the least bit.

Paul warned, "Let no corrupt communication proceed out of your mouth, but that which is good to the use of edifying" (Ephesians 4:29). This includes all singing.

God's holy indignation against Israel was made known to the prophet Malachi. The prophet asked the people of the Lord, "If ye offer the blind for sacrifice, is it not evil? and if ye offer the lame and sick, is it not evil?" (Malachi 1:8). God was not about to accept from their hands a corrupt sacrifice to His glory. "Ye brought that which was torn, and the lame, and the sick; thus ye brought an offering: should I accept this of your hand? saith the Lord" (Malachi 1:13).

They knew their offerings were to be pure and spot-less—but they had sunk so low in their adoration for God, they took to Him a sacrifice of corruption. And a horrible curse follows such disobedience. "But cursed be the deceiver, which hath in his flock a male, and voweth, and sacrificeth unto the Lord a corrupt thing: for I am a great King, saith the Lord of hosts, and my name is dreadful among the heathen" (Malachi 1:14).

God calls him a deceiver who has in his repertoire the music born in the womb of holiness, music that is pure and praiseworthy, but who puts it aside and offers to the Lord the corrupt sacrifices of music out of an evil womb. God is saying here, "I am a mighty and glorious King, worthy only of the best, most spiritual, godly music you are capable of offering. All else is corrupt sacrifice." It truly bothers me that the rockers will have one or two deeply spiritual songs on their albums, and the rest is the harsh, grating music of rock. They know how to do it right and acceptable to the Lord. Some of the rock performers tell me, "I really don't like it myself, but the kids do. I do it to attract the youth." My answer—"What about Him? Will you desecrate the offering to please the crowd?"

I hear sincere Christians say, "Satan doesn't own

music. It belongs to God. The music doesn't matter as long as the words are right." Dead wrong! The devil owns all music that is ungodly and evil. And Satan had all the right words when he tempted Christ. The Israelites dancing around the golden calf had all the right words. Were they not singing, "This is the god that brought us out of Egypt"? Same people, same music, same words—but their god had changed. It is much more than holy, intelligent words. Satan has always spoken in temptation with accurate words mingled with a lot of Scripture, and so has every angel of light who has come to deceive.

Rock music was born with more than a particular sound; it was conceived by a spirit, and it continues to be activated by that same spirit that gave birth to it. It is the spirit of Antichrist; and the more one becomes wholly devoted to Jesus Christ, the more readily he discerns that spirit. I do not know of a single true worshipper of the Lord Jesus Christ who desires to offer rock music as an offering to a holy God.

I've noticed that musicians at Christian concerts seldom perform rock just before the message and invitation. It is not conducive to conviction of any kind because it is of another spirit. If it is of God, why not use it before the invitation? Why not a ripping rock segment just before the sermonette? It is reserved for the entertainment part of concerts, to the accompanying of fleshy whistles, shouting, and grooving. It doesn't inspire them to kneel and pray, or even to bow their heads and worship. There is not one ounce of conviction in it—God refuses to touch it. What it does is turn audiences on to a fleshly display of jumping on seats, jiving and dancing in anything but a spiritual manner.

All music not conceived in the womb of the Holy Ghost is unsuitable as an offering in the house of the Lord. It is unacceptable to Him as King, ruling and reigning in this body, which is His temple. I don't care who borrows music from the devil's womb, including ancient fathers; God will not accept a sacrifice that was taken from the devil's altars and placed upon Christ's sacred altar. But keep in mind there is a vast difference between borrowing a tune and borrowing a style of music. Rock is more than music—it is a lifestyle. Why should we give the Lord the devil's hand-me-downs? Why not original, pure music for the King of Kings?

I once thought God would accept rock music from those who didn't know better or from those who knew no other kind of music, and I even wrote a tract in defense of their actions. But now I see differently. I was dead wrong. Our God is so great, so holy, so mighty and powerful and glorious—we dare not bring to Him anything tainted or polluted by sin. His eyes are too pure; His holiness too majestic to offer Him any kind of music still being offered to Satan in rock concerts worldwide. We know how to offer Him a pure and holy sacrifice without a spot or blemish. There is not a Christian singer or group alive who does not know how to offer the Lord music born of the Spirit. Sadly, many of them stubbornly bring to Him that which is blind, sick, and corrupt, simply to attract crowds, sell records, become popular, and be considered contemporary. A curse follows that kind of evil work. "Take thou away from me the noise of thy songs; for I will not hear the melody of thy viols. But ye have borne the tabernacle of your Moloch and Chiun your images, the star of your god, which ye made to yourselves" (Amos 5:23,26).

3. God has His prescribed boundaries for worship.

Malachi said, "Ye offer polluted bread upon mine altar; and ye say, Wherein have we polluted thee? In that ye say, The table of the Lord is contemptible"

(Malachi 1:7). "But ye have profaned it, in that ye say, The table of the Lord is polluted; and the fruit thereof, even his meat, is contemptible" (Malachi 1:12).

The meaning is not complicated, and it has everything to do with the attitude of rock musicians and their devoted fans. There is an attitude among rock fans who are Christian that truly frightens me. They become sold out to it; they promote it with zeal; they will not give it up, not even for Jesus and the Holy Ghost—it is that deeply imbedded in their hearts. They refuse to depart from the "snare of death" (Proverbs 13:14).

I am as much concerned about the attitude of Christians devoted to rock as the music itself. They are like the children who mocked Elijah, taunting him, "Go up baldy—old man!" (2 Kings 2:23). They won't even listen to a man come from God. It matters not to them that he has been shut in with God for weeks, or that he is pure in heart, or that he has truly heard the very heart and mind of God on the subject. David said, "Let the righteous smite me; it shall be a kindness; and let him reprove me; it shall be an excellent oil, which shall not break my head" (Psalm 141:5). But these Christian youth devoted to rock would even wave off angels. It truly scares me! "Because I knew that thou art obstinate, and thy neck is an iron sinew, and thy brow brass" (Isaiah 48:4). It makes me know there is an evil spirit behind it, lying spirits causing strong delusions, causing many to be given over to a lie. "I also will choose their delusions, and will bring their fears upon them; because when I called, none did answer; when I spake, they did not hear: but they did evil before mine eyes, and chose that in which I delighted not" (Isaiah 66:4). Even this chapter angers them. To them I am just a misinformed old fogey, out of touch with reality. They say I am "culture bound" to an old generation.

Think of what I am saying, young people. Stop a minute and ask yourself, "Why am I so bothered? Why am I so defensive of this music? Could he be right—am I deceived and under the bondage of a lying spirit?" "O that thou hadst hearkened to my commandments! Then had thy peace been as a river, and thy righteousness as the waves of the sea" (Isaiah 48:18).

What Is Meant by the Table Of the Lord?

We must know, because God's wrath has been revealed from heaven against Christians who think it is contemptible. Contemptible here means: boring, beneath me, unacceptable, to look down upon, to detest, snub, recoil from with pride. What then is it in God's house, this table of the Lord, that so many recoil from with pride and detest and consider boring?

The table of the Lord implies The Lord's Meal. David said, "Thou preparest a table before me in the presence of mine enemies" (Psalm 23:5). That was a feast, a celestial meal. God commanded Israel, "Thou shalt set upon the table shewbread before me alway" (Exodus 25:30). The table was to have on it twelve loaves, to be renewed weekly on the Sabbath day. They constituted a continual thank offering to God, and it was referred to as the bread of "presence," signifying God's presence in the holy of holies. Wine and frankincense were offered with the bread.

The offering on the table of the Lord was not acceptable unless the surroundings were holy, the flour the finest, and the frankincense pure. The table was overlaid with pure gold. Nothing common or unclean was to ever touch that sacred table. The "meal of the Lord" represented what the people brought to the Lord of their labors and worship. The sweet smelling savor of the pure frankincense wafted to God as an acceptable offering on His table. The holy bread, touched by no unclean hand, was the Lord's—His feast. It was to be offered willingly, out of a heart of love and obedience. Once it was offered to God, the priests ate it before replacing it with fresh loaves. It represents Christ, the living Word, with life-giving energy.

I ask you, young people, can you go to the Lord's table and offer to Him the bread of rock? Is it pure, untouched by corruption? Do you truly believe He will accept such an offering? Hardly! What kind of "meal" are you serving the Lord?

But this generation is bored of "speaking to yourselves in psalms and hymns and spiritual songs, singing and making melody in your heart to the Lord" (Ephesians 5:19). Hymns? Spiritual songs? Sweet melodies? Not if a new breed of musicians have their way. They actually laugh at Paul's description of good, Christ-exalting music, as described here in Ephesians. "But they rebelled, and vexed his holy Spirit: therefore he was turned to be their enemy, and he fought against them" (Isaiah 63:10).

God says to this generation, "You rejected the holy hymns, the sweet melodies, the sanctified sound of joy and pure gladness! You detested the music of your fathers who worshipped in purity. It was your disdaining pride of all that was old. You want the miracles of the book of Acts, but not the purity of the fathers. You recoiled from the music born of the Spirit and embraced the music of this world."

4. God is looking for overcomers who will search out the old paths and find the right way.

Please, in the name of all that is sacred and holy in the eyes of God, hear these words of the prophet Jeremiah. "Thus saith the Lord, Stand ye in the ways, and see, and ask for the old paths, where is the good way, and walk therein, and ye shall find rest for your souls. But they said, We will not walk therein" (Jeremiah 6:16). Not that the old songs and hymns are to be used exclusively, but they should not be cast aside and replaced with anything light and shallow.

Also, please listen to the godly watchmen the Lord sends to blow the trumpet to warn of danger and God's displeasure. "Also I set watchmen over you, saying, Hearken to the sound of the trumpet. But they said, We will not hearken" (Jeremiah 6:17). God raises up watchmen to "reprove the works of darkness" (Ephesians 5:11).

This writer is one of His watchmen set by God on the wall of this nation, and this message is a TRUMPET CALL to heed the Lord's message. Most, just as Jeremiah predicted, will not hearken. Their ears and hearts are closed; they are married to their music and will not hear what the Spirit is saying. Isaiah warned against "children" who agree among them to sin. "Woe to the rebellious children, saith the Lord, that take counsel, but not of me; and that cover with a covering, but not of my spirit, that they may add sin to sin" (Isaiah 30:1).

The Spirit is saying, "Take a bold step out of your rut; check out the old ways, the old hymns, the music of your holy fathers, and at least listen to their message. Their songs have a pure doctrine, something badly needed today. Get on your face before God and seek a revelation of what is right, of what truly pleases heaven. Discover good, pure, sanctified music and walk in it. Never again bring to the King of Glory a corrupt thing. Do it your Lord's way and you will find great peace and rest for your soul. Otherwise, turmoil and grief."

I weary of rock advocates telling me it gets results; that it draws the unconverted. That has been a Roman

Catholic argument for centuries, as they justify their missionaries who mix pagan worship and traditions with their gospel. It does not produce heart changes! The Pharisees sought converts, but they turned them into children of darkness twice over. You can't feed poison to babies without disaster. Only the pure fruit will pass the test at the judgment seat.

There is a tendency today to bless and embrace anything as long as there is sincerity and the name of Jesus is prominent. How dangerous! Not everyone who says, "Jesus, Jesus" will enter heaven. Some are workers of iniquity, totally unknown by the Lord Jesus. What evil, corrupt manners and methods now adopted simply to draw a crowd.

Out of the Abundance of the Heart

That which is in the heart comes out the mouth. Out of a pure heart will flow pure music, and out of a divided heart will flow music that is tainted. Pure and impure water cannot flow out of the same fountain, and holy and unholy music cannot pour out of a clean heart.

God is more concerned about the hearts and lives of those who perform and listen to the music of the world. If the heart is not clean before God, everything that comes out of the mouth is corrupt. The sweetest, most Christ-exalting song coming out of a sinful, rebellious heart is an abomination to God. A teenager may listen to only majestic hymns and melodious psalms, but if the heart and the ears are not pure before God—he or she may as well be listening to the wildest punk rock in the land.

A performer, or a group of performers, may present only the best repertoire of the old gold songs of the church—but if there is secret sin harbored in their hearts, or evil thoughts and fleshly ambition, their music is as corrupt as the hard rockers.

Man looks on the outward appearance, but God looks on the heart. Yet the outward appearance is the fruit of the tree that grows within the heart.

What is in the heart of the rock lovers and promoters? That is the question God is most concerned with. Is there rebellion? Is there a lingering love for this world? Is there a desire to have the music of the world, no matter how evil, and still have a hope of heaven? I have observed that many of the very young rock enthusiasts are going through a stage of rebellion. Their music simply reflects the turmoil and despair within. God Himself could not get them to give up their rock idol.

I have also observed that performers and groups that feature rock, especially hard rock, have no ringing testimony of holiness and separation from the world. Many still drink, especially wine and beer. Some still sneak their pot, cocaine, and other drugs. Others are sexually promiscuous. The harder their rock, the more compromising they are. I can listen to their music and tell in the Spirit immediately what their secret lives are like.

God is saying something very powerful to all who will listen. He is looking at what you have become, and not only at what you sing and perform. What about it—singers, musicians, bands, groups? Are you truly broken before the Lord, and are you spending hours in His holy presence to allow the Holy Spirit to dig down deep into the hidden recesses of your heart? Are you calling on His name, diligently searching His Word, obeying Him in everything in your life? Are you absolutely positive that all you are doing on stage is edifying, Christ-exalting, and holy? Or, do you soak in the applause, turn the kids on, and go for the thunderous response to your talent? Is the flesh on parade? Are you using Jesus as a stepping stone to secular success? Have you seen Jesus sitting in the front seat, and can He stay for the whole program? Is there a root of pride in you; do you compare yourself with others; do you think you are special and unique? God judges motives! There is so much showing off at Christian concerts. So many performers want the respect of secular musicians, so they go as far as they can and simply call it Jesus music. It's a big sham! They ought to quit using Jesus as a ticket to fame and go full time into secular rock. For some it is just a small step.

What about the record and tape buyers, the concert goers, and the radio listeners? Can you truly worship Christ to rock tunes? Is rock feeding something in you, very deep, very subtle, something you can't put your finger on? Are you positive that Jesus Christ the Lord is King in your life and that He means more to you than even rock music? If He asked you to give up rock music, would you?

I am asking these important questions for a reason. The church of Jesus Christ is asleep. Its shepherds are mostly slumbering or chasing after their own dreams. Only a sleeping church could have allowed the abominations now poisoning it. The nation is about to fall under horrible judgments, and things are soon going to shake and crumble. There will be panic and hysteria on all sides. In the midst of all this, God is going to raise up a holy, overcoming remnant—and many of them will be young people. The Lord is getting His bride ready for wedding night. We are soon going home to be with Him. All things are now ready, Christ has already risen from His chamber and soon He will be united with His bride.

What kind of music will we be singing as we go out to meet Him? Will it be the shout of victory, holiness, joy in the Lord—or will it be an echo from some heathen concert hall? When you know you will soon be in paradise, what song should be on your lips? Seeing that all things are going to burn and all the elements will melt with intense heat, what kind of persons should we be in all holy conversation and singing?

Put yourself, in your mind, at the last hour of time, the last hour you will spend on earth. In less than one hour you will be looking in His glorious face. You will be singing with the martyrs who had their heads chopped off for being true to Jesus. Angel choirs will join you. You will see and hear instruments never seen before, and players who are seraphims. Cherubs will add their voices. I ask you—what kind of music will it be then? Will it sound like rock? Will you suddenly have to change your style, or do you even now hang your head and confess, I don't know the sound of glory yet. When you see the Lord, will He bless your song? Maybe you've been flooding your soul with the wrong music! As for me, I am singing right now the songs I'll sing then, to a music that will not be strange over there. It is a simple song of adoration and worship to my holy and precious Savior.

Judgment Against Rock
In God's House

God holds the keys of life and death, and He was making a powerful statement when He claimed the lives of rockers like Jimi Hendrix, Janice Joplin, Elvis Presley, and John Lennon. They were silenced. The king of rock was taken away! They are dead!

If judgment begins in the house of God, what chance is there that such wickedness can long remain unpunished? If death is ministered so swiftly outside His house, how tragic will it be when He comes suddenly to His own house to judge and to purge. He will lay the ax to the root! He will blow away all the chaff and let remain only the wheat. We are about to see some awesome judgment on these abominations. Go ahead and serve your god of rock, but to do so you are forsaking His holiness and are opening yourself to judgment. "If ye forsake the Lord, and serve strange gods, then he will turn and do you hurt, and consume you, after that he hath done you good" (Joshua 24:20). I am not calling up Old Testament curses—these are moral principles of judgment seen all through the Word of God.

In recent months, even the most avid rock advocates have been revolted by what is called Christian punk rock. "They've gone too far—they're too much!" they say. But what did you expect; where did you think it would end? It ends in ridiculous, outrageous, flaunted mimicry of hell itself. It's the root of the same tree; all the Holy Spirit has done is expose its very roots so its fruit could be clearly identified. "Wherefore, as I live, saith the Lord God; Surely, because thou hast defiled my sanctuary with all thy detestable things, and with all thine abominations, therefore will I also diminish thee: neither shall mine eye spare, neither will I have any pity" (Ezekiel 5:11).

Out of God's house, all you rock showmen—with your light shows, your painted, rebellious faces, your bizarre costumes! Out—you mockers of all that is sacred and holy! Out with your confusing words, light and silly crossover songs, and calling Jesus, "You"! Out with the jiving, the blasphemy of turning eternal salvation into a fleshly party. Go ahead—"Party with Jesus"—but soon you will face the Judge who sentenced Jimi Hendrix, Janice Joplin, Elvis Presley, and John Lennon. They partied and rocked their way to hell, and you refused to learn from their tragedies.

To Christian young people who are admirers of these groups and their music, please hear me. This is no longer fun and games. There is nothing innocent or harmless about this kind of iniquity. "A companion of fools shall be destroyed" (Proverbs 13:20). You are playing with supernatural fire; you are flirting with principalities and powers of darkness. Some of them are angels of light sent to deceive. Some are under the direction of lying spirits from hell and don't know it. They say they are believers, but they preach another Jesus. Even the devil believes, and he trembles at the name of Christ. They are breaking one of the clearest commandments ever given, and they seek to bring you into their disobedience. Paul warned: "Be ye not unequally yoked together with unbelievers: for what fellowship hath righteousness with unrighteousness? And what communion hath light with darkness? And what concord hath Christ with Belial? Or what part hath he that believeth with an infidel? And what agreement hath the temple of God with idols? For ye are the temple of the living God; as God hath said, I will dwell in them; and I will be their God, and they shall be my people. Wherefore come out from among them, and be ye separate, saith the Lord, and touch not the unclean thing; and I will receive you, and will be a Father unto you, and ye shall be my sons and daughters, saith the Lord Almighty" (2 Corinthians 6:14-18).

"No One—Nothing Strange—in My Sanctuary"

"They please themselves in the children of strangers" (Isaiah 2:6).

Is this matter a joke to God? On the contrary! His wrath boils against anyone or anything in His house that is strange or abominable. The prophet Ezekiel warned Israel, "You introduced strangers, uncircumcised of heart, to be in my sanctuary to pollute it, even my house. You broke my covenant with all your abominations. You placed keepers in my house for yourselves...because they ministered unto them before their idols, and were a stumbling block of iniquity unto the house of Israel; therefore have I lifted up mine hand against them, saith the Lord Jehovah, and they shall bear their iniquity. And they shall not approach to me....They shall bear their disgrace" (Ezekiel 44:7-13 Spurrell).

That is a frightful Old Testament prophecy that needs to be heard today: "You introduced strangers, doing strange things in my house, corrupted God's people, even though they minister not to the Lord, but to their own idols; I will lift up my hand against this horrid thing. I don't even know them; they will pay for disgracing Me!" Read it! It's all there. It happened once in Israel, but it is a dual prophecy about to happen again—judgment upon all the strange, abominable music of devils in His sanctuary. Sudden death! On the spot! It happened in a New Testament church to Ananias and Sapphira—it could happen again. You can't fool with the Holy Ghost! You can't keep back part of the price of full surrender and separation.

There Can Be No Worship If the Names of Baalim Be on Our Lips

"I will take away the names of Baalim out of her mouth" (Hosea 2:17).

God is saying, "My true worshippers will never again ever speak of, let alone do, those things that represent the old life and former idols." Baal, Babel, and Babylon are theologically synonymous in the Bible. They represent confusion, mixture, mastery, possession. Baalim is plural and refers to all the names of the false gods integrated with Baal worship.

Satan has succeeded in bringing into God's house the men and the music of confusion and mixture, which is used to bring souls under mastery to the demon god Baal. Hosea prophesied God is going to raise up a body of purified saints, dead to the world, whose lips will never again mention the names of anyone or anything pertaining to Baalim, the god of mixture and confusion who seeks to possess.

I walk into a Christian bookstore, look over the record jackets, and think I'm back on Times Square in a punk rock music center. Have you seen those covers lately? They are poor copies of wild, secular garbage. I've seen wicked sinners blush and walk away, saying, "That's religious? Wow, who'd ever thought it! What's the world coming to?" The so-called Christian rock groups look like freaks, with demonic and witch-like expressions. They put serpents and other grotesque creatures on their jackets. They are reflections out of hell itself.

Not only is the false god Baal behind it, not only is it demonic; much of it, I believe, has been conjured in homosexual minds under the influence of cocaine and other drugs. What do you see, but mixture and confusion—the outright expressions of a satanic deity! The Christian music business is becoming, on the whole, more vile and corrupt than the secular. How Satan must rejoice as they fall under his influence. They now try to compete to see who can go the farthest into the secular garbage heap and peddle the filth of the world. A devoted, Christ-loving musician cannot be associated with a music business infiltrated by the powers of darkness.

I say, on the authority of God's Word through the prophets, it is impossible to be in union with Christ and even mention that filth. "Howbeit I sent unto you all my servants the prophets, rising early and sending them, saying, Oh, do not this abominable thing that I hate" (Jeremiah 44:4). Only despisers of the Lord Jesus could embrace what He hates. Only the rebellious could purchase one of their records. Only those with a divided heart could go to one of their concerts or view one of their video cassettes. Their video cassettes are demonic and blasphemous. The spirit of mixture and confusion it was born in will slowly possess you and lead you blindly to the altars of Baal. Sneer if you choose, but you have been warned.

The church is too weak now to purge itself of all the abominable music polluting God's house. So I believe God is going to clean it up and judge it sovereignly, on His own. He has promised to appear in Zion in holy anger and purge His floor. He will smite and make examples of some of the worst perpetrators. He will raise up a discerning, spiritual body of true worshippers who will utterly reject all music of the golden calf. The time is not far off when the rockers will lose their Christian crowds. Their following will dwindle and die. Jesus, as He once did with the money changers in the temple, will drive out of His house all the cheap showmanship, the punk clowns, the covetous producers, the gay performers, the hype and sensationalism, the light shows, and all the children of darkness posing as the children of light. That music will continue in the temples of sin and compromise but will die in the hearts and temples of the pure and undefiled. Those who continue indulging in the music of devils will get worse and more like their worldly heroes; the music will get wilder, the concerts more rebellious, and those who attend will be only the fake believers. So-called "punk Christian" concerts will be demonic in character and will be attended solely by those who serve another Christ—a false Christ. All true worshippers will forsake them and leave them only with the backslidden and lukewarm.

If you don't believe anything else I've prophesied,

believe this: God is going to clean up the music in His
house! The rockers' and punkers' free ride on Jesus is
over! The Holy Ghost is determined to see that Christ
is worshipped in Spirit and in truth—and not through
demonic channels. "So shall my word be that goeth
forth out of my mouth: it shall not return unto me void,
but it shall accomplish that which I please, and it shall
prosper in the thing whereto I sent it" (Isaiah 55:11).

It Comes Down Finally to Our Love for Christ

"If any man love the world, or the things that are of
the world, the love of the Father is not in him" (1 John
2:15).

What other argument do we need? It all comes down
to our love for Jesus Christ. Does our love for Him mean
more to us than all those things of the world, including
its music? If you are made to feel the grief of His heart
against all that is tainted by this world, would not your
love for Him make you avoid it like a plague? I say yes.

The only reason these worldly things have flourished
among us has been due to our cold love. The love of
many waxed cold—so iniquity easily made inroads.
Get back to fervent love for Jesus and you won't need
someone like me condemning and pointing out sin. You
will know it, because your love for Jesus will reveal it to
you.

If, in eternity, we are known as the most wicked of all
generations, then it will mean we loved Jesus Christ
the least. God help us!

God didn't tell me to expect results from this particular chapter—all He told me to do was sound a trumpet and warn Christians that God is going to spew out
of His true church all music of devils. Just as Isaiah
was sent to warn Israel and make her hard, I feel God
has sent me to warn the youth—so some will repent,

but others will harden themselves and be judged. "And he said, Go, and tell this people, Hear ye indeed, but understand not; and see ye indeed, but perceive not. Make the heart of this people fat, and make their ears heavy, and shut their eyes; lest they see with their eyes, and hear with their ears, and understand with their heart, and convert, and be healed" (Isaiah 6:9,10). "And they, whether they will hear, or whether they will forbear, (for they are a rebellious house,) yet shall know that there hath been a prophet among them" (Ezekiel 2:5). "Son of man, I have made thee a watchman unto the house of Israel: therefore hear the word at my mouth, and give them warning from me" (Ezekiel 3:17).

If we are going to line up with God, we need to stand up against rock, help pray it down, and refuse to support any Christian performer or group or station who continues pushing it.

A Word for Spiritual Musicians And Spiritual Music Lovers Only!

Those who are spiritual and growing in the knowledge of the Lord Jesus Christ are developing their spiritual senses and are gaining new powers of discernment. As they hunger and thirst for righteousness and spend much time in prayer and study of God's Word, they can quickly recognize music that has been borrowed from the realm of darkness. Devoted lovers of Jesus Christ can discern when a singer or group has copied its style and music from a secular rock group. They can tell when a performer or group is in the Spirit or in the flesh. There is always a clear witness of the Holy Spirit on that which is godly and pure. There is also a strong check, an inner grief, when the music is tainted by evil.

Without exception, I have noticed that all who go deep in the Lord and who become devoted worshippers, spending much time in the secret closet of prayer, begin to reject all harsh, pounding, frivolous music. They hunger for music that soothes the soul and complements the rest God gives to the inner man. They respond only to that music that lifts up the lovely name of Jesus, and that inspires toward a broken heart and a contrite spirit. It can be loud or soft, slow or fast, but the music that touches the soul of the spiritual person is not the thrashing sound of rock.

Show me a weeping, praying, humble, Christ-seeking musician, and I'll show you one who will stick to Holy Ghost anointed music—at all costs. That musician, or group, would rather be unknown and forgotten than grieve the Holy Spirit by going with the careless, backslidden crowd. Rock music would die in one week in gospel circles if every musician got broken before the Lord, receiving a vision of the awesome holiness of God.

The spiritual understand what I am saying. I am not saying that giving up worldly music can save anyone. Again I say, we are saved by grace alone, and not by good works. This message is about obedience from a heart of love. We get our security at the bloodstained altar, but our cleansing at the laver. We are cleansed by the holy Word of God. May God cleanse us all!

Chapter 5
The Building of Temples

"For Israel hath forgotten his Maker, and buildeth temples; and Judah hath multiplied fenced cities: but I will send a fire upon his cities, and it shall devour the palaces thereof" (Hosea 8:14).

I tremble at what God has called upon me to prophesy and denounce in this chapter—the building of cities and temples. Hosea prophesied against men of God who thought they were building sanctuaries, but Jehovah looked upon them as sepulchers.

What a pathetic word-picture of the dead ritualism among God's people, "They forgot God and built Him cities and temples." History repeats itself, and it is happening all over again. The nation is about to fall, and men of God are off chasing dreams.

The prophet Hosea declared that God would come against His house like a "screaming eagle," upon those who were crying out to Him—"My God, we know thee" (Hosea 8:1,2). But these men who claimed to know God, these builders of cities and temples, had "cast off the thing that is good," and they were actually being "chased by the enemy" into projects that were an abomination to Jehovah (Hosea 8:3). They were being led by lying spirits.

The builders of temples had become to God as "vessels wherein is no pleasure" (Hosea 8:8). Whereas they spent their time, energy, and effort building their cities and temples, the prophet Ezekiel cried out that they were building for themselves. "Woe, woe unto thee! saith the Lord God; that thou hast built unto thee an eminent place, and hast made thee an high place in every street" (Ezekiel 16:23,24).

While they were busy building their cities, dreams, and temples, God said His true house was being neglected. Jeremiah expressed God's grief over such twisted values—"Truly this is a grief, and I must bear it. My tabernacle is spoiled, and all my cords are broken: my children are gone forth of me, and they are not: there is none to stretch forth my tent any more, and to set up my curtains. For the pastors are become brutish, and have not sought the Lord: therefore they shall not prosper, and all their flocks shall be scattered" (Jeremiah 10:19-21).

What a horrifying indictment from the grief-stricken heart of God. Pastors and evangelists, without wisdom, spending their time building their own material brick and stone temples—and in the process, wounding and scattering sheep and neglecting the true temple, the one not made with human hands.

"Solomon built him an house. Howbeit the most High dwelleth not in temples made with hands...What house hath ye built me?" (Acts 7:47-49). Paul said, "What? know ye not that your body is the temple of the Holy Ghost which is in you, which ye have of God?" (1 Corinthians 6:19). Also, "But Christ as a son over his own house; whose house are we" (Hebrews 3:6).

It is the grief of God and it would have been a horror to Paul, this stupid race to build costly, overlarge churches, towers, cities, resort hotels, Christian playgrounds, and recreation centers. Men of God are building the wrong buildings! God's cry is, "Who will

stretch forth my tent? Who will set up my curtains?"
(Jeremiah 10:20).

Everything men of God build today, they do "to the
glory of God," so it is said. But how do we add glory to
Him who already has all the glory?

Does God get glory when His servants build their
temples on robbery? God said, "I hate robbery for burnt
offering" (Isaiah 61:8). God is robbed of precious time
that belongs to Him. All those hours spent poring over
plans, spent on site, spent raising money, spent running about—should have been spent in prayer and the
study of God's Word. Men of God are supposed to give
themselves to prayer and the Word, and anything that
hinders that commitment is robbery.

Does God get glory when a shepherd has to fleece the
sheep to build his dream project, then keep fleecing
them to keep it afloat? This is a very serious matter in
the Lord's eyes, and no man of God can throw aside His
awesome warnings about shepherds who overburden
sheep. I hear the pitiful bleatings of overburdened
sheep from one end of this nation to the other. Isaiah
called it, grinding the face of the poor. "What mean ye
that ye beat my people to pieces, and grind the faces of
the poor, saith the Lord God of hosts" (Isaiah 3:15).

Jeremiah wept, "Mine heart within me is broken
because of the prophets; all my bones shake; I am like
a drunken man...because of the words of his holiness"
(Jeremiah 23:9). Joel lamented, "The flocks of sheep are
made desolate" (Joel 1:18). Isaiah has the worst indictment of all against these greedy shepherds, with
words that make me blush: "His watchmen are blind:
they are all ignorant, they are all dumb dogs, they cannot bark; sleeping, lying down, loving to slumber. Yea,
they are greedy dogs which can never have enough, and
they are shepherds that cannot understand: they all
look to their own way, every one for his gain, from his

quarter" (Isaiah 56:10,11).

This prophet's anger was so hot against self-seeking shepherds because they were so occupied doing their own thing, building their own projects while "the righteous perisheth, and no man layeth it to heart: and kind men are taken away" (Isaiah 57:1).

Think of it—kind sheep! Righteous people perishing! Not just the wicked, but the merciful and kind. And why? The shepherds were all wrapped up in their own dreams and neglected the sheep. If men of God were half as interested in people's needs and in a revival of holiness as in building some great new project, this could not happen. Jeremiah said, "My people hath been lost sheep: their shepherds have caused them to go astray, they have turned them away on the mountains: they have gone from mountain to hill, they have forgotten their restingplace" (Jeremiah 50:6).

The shepherd who is building a temple or project without a true mandate from God is feeding himself with the fat of the flock. And God won't permit it—He has thundered his anger against it through all the prophets. Ezekiel warned, "Son of man, prophesy against the shepherds of Israel, prophesy, and say unto them, Thus saith the Lord God unto the shepherds; Woe be to the shepherds of Israel that do feed themselves! should not the shepherds feed the flocks? Ye eat the fat, and ye clothe you with the wool, ye kill them that are fed: but ye feed not the flock" (Ezekiel 34:2,3).

I go to certain towns and cities where there is great unemployment, and those who are working, so underpaid. There is hardship on every hand; the elderly hardly have enough to eat; farmers are losing their farms; and people are going bankrupt. Yet, unbelievably, there is a pastor in that town or city building himself a monstrous temple. His people love him, and he tells them God told him they must build. And build he does—with no one daring to stop him. I see all those dear hurting, struggling sheep in that congregation, just so much meat to feed that shepherd's dream; and I hear ringing in my ears these horrific words—"O ye shepherds, hear the word of the Lord; thus saith the Lord God; Behold I am against the shepherds; and I will require my flock at their hand, and cause them to cease from feeding the flock; neither shall the shepherds feed themselves any more; for I will deliver my flock from their mouth, that they may not be meat for them" (Ezekiel 34:9,10).

I heard a television evangelist trying to justify his multimillion dollar, spanking new, expensive building project. In so many words he was saying, "You may be very poor and you may have to borrow to send me your gift, but God will make it up to you." Ezekiel called it a "conspiracy of her prophets." "There is a conspiracy of her prophets in the midst thereof, like a roaring lion ravening the prey; they have devoured souls; they have taken the treasure and precious things; they have made her many widows in the midst thereof" (Ezekiel 22:25).

When I hear these pitiful appeals, the unbelievable justifications, the pressuring of even the poorest of Christians for money, I hear the words of the prophet Zechariah ringing in my ears, "Their own shepherds pity them not" (Zechariah 11:5). Habakkuk said, "Woe to him that buildeth a town with blood, and stablisheth a city by iniquity! Behold, is it not of the Lord of hosts that the people shall labour in the very fire, and the people shall weary themselves for very vanity?" (Habakkuk 2:12,13).

The very holiness of God is affronted by shepherds who use God's Word as a club to extract money. Jeremiah said, "Cursed is he that doeth the work of the Lord deceitfully" (Jeremiah 48:10). Oh, how the Scrip-

tures are twisted, taken out of context, used and misused to scare or bribe the sheep into building the
wrong house. Even worse, shepherds often take advan-
tage of the love and respect their flocks have for them.
"But this is a people robbed and spoiled; they are all of
them snared in holes, and they are hid in prison houses: they are for a prey, and none delivereth; for a spoil,
and none saith, Restore. Who among you will give ear
to this? Who will hearken and hear for the time to
come?" (Isaiah 42:22,23).

Where's the Fire?

I have a question. If we have built to the Lord these
magnificent new altars, where is the fire? Elijah built!
He built an altar to God's glory and the consuming fire
of God fell and shook the nation. The heathen crowds
were stunned; they fell on their faces in terror.

God displayed His great favor for the altar constructed by Elijah. He answered by fire. Why isn't God
answering by fire on our great new altars? Why aren't
our heathen neighbors aware of some awesome thing
God is doing at our newly constructed altars? Is God
going to pour out His holy fire on our resorts, playgrounds, and tourist attractions?

We build these great, expansive altars, but there is
no prophet of God there to call down the fire on them.
Again, I ask—Where is the fire? It makes me wonder if
God is displeased. Why won't He answer with that consuming fire that fell on every altar in past times with
which He was pleased? Why is there no word or fire
from heaven?

We call in big-name evangelists to fill up our huge
new auditoriums—hoping they will pack them out and
justify their existence. But where's the fire?

We call in the minstrels; we call in the showmen; we
call in producers and performers of great spectacles.

We get the crowds occasionally. But where's the fire? What some men of God won't do, what compromises they will make—all to get the crowd in.

We'll build our temples to accommodate the crowds but not the fire. If God's consuming fire did fall on some of these magnificent temples, it would probably empty them of the crowds and leave only the sanctified few who cleave to the Lord. Out would go all the two-timing adulterers; the lovers of pleasure more than the lovers of God; the backslidden deacons and elders who love their secret sins; the drinkers, smokers, and party types; the lukewarm who love soft preaching—none of them could stand before the holy, consuming fire.

Maybe then God could come back to those altars and build Himself a glorious new body without spot or wrinkle. Maybe the day will come when the crowds don't matter at all, but all that will be important is the continually burning fire on the altar—continually sanctifying all who draw near.

Lord, send the fire! Sweep through all these big, dead, dry sanctuaries and purge the whole thing. Straighten up our values! Shut down and bankrupt all the abominable playthings and religious toys and ego-centric dreams. Burn out the pride and the worldliness! Pluck sin out by the roots. Do away with all the showmanship, gaudiness, and worldliness. Expose adultery and fornication! Make it hot—make it like an oven—and consume, consume, consume us!

God Says, "I Can't Afford Them Anymore."

When I prayed about the building of temples and expensive projects, I continually felt a certain grief in my heart but couldn't discover the reason. I know it was the Lord who whispered to my heart, "I can't afford these building programs anymore."

It has to do with more than money; it has to do with the high cost upon some of His most favored servants. Many of those building today are among His strongest warriors—men of tremendous faith and compassion for human need. It has taken too high a toll on their spiritual and physical well-being. In fact, some have gone too far and will never recover the anointing they once had.

These are the men of God so much needed on the front lines, pulling down satanic strongholds, delivering the searing Word of God to a slumbering church. They should be the men shut in with God in the secret closet, hours and days on end, growing deep and strong in the vision of His holiness, and giving themselves wholly to prayer and the study of God's Word. Had many of these talented men of God done that, rather than get straddled with projects, they would have been spiritual giants by now—shaking multitudes for God.

God can no longer afford to see His mightiest men strapped under such suffocating financial pressure and wasting time on frivolous toy projects. Time that should be spent in worship, in beholding His face, and in being changed from glory to glory is being spent pounding the gates of heaven for money to finish or carry on some great enterprise—much of it nonessential. Time that should have been invested in devouring God's Word, in hearing from heaven, and in getting the true mind of the Lord is spent in organization and planning. The spiritual, mental drain is a grief to God's heart.

I look into the drawn faces of many great men of God involved in massive projects, and my heart goes out to them. Many do not sleep well anymore; they are in so deep, and no end seems to be in sight. It has to be very distracting to their quiet time with the Lord. It has to be disheartening, not to be able to give the Lord the time needed to keep a fresh anointing. And if he is truly a man of God, he is never satisfied to give the sheep scraps. It is one of the worst abominations in the eyes of God for one of His pastors or evangelists to rush into the pulpit unprepared, having no ringing word of authority or power.

I believe the Holy Spirit is calling His great warriors back to their knees. The time comes when God will ask—Do you go on with Me, or with continual projects?

I visit beautiful new houses of God, nearly finished. I breathe a sigh of relief for that dear man of God who undertook it. "Now," I say to myself, "he is free to get back to intense prayer and to grow deeper in truth and revelation." But that's often not the case. I am taken into his office and shown plans for his other ambitious projects. Retirement centers, recreation facilities, schools—and I leave with my head spinning. I ask myself, "Is that dear man going to spend the rest of his life building? When will he ever be satisfied to simply preach and minister to the Lord?"

No, God really can't afford this continual building of temples and institutions. Men of vision are now needed on the spiritual front. There is a desperate need for a ministry that is moving in a new realm of spiritual authority—and that can happen only through a kind of devotion and separation not yet seen among us.

Men of God, finish what you've started. Call a halt to all the rest, and tell your people that from now on you will shut yourself in with God so you can stand in the pulpit with a powerful "thus saith the Lord." You don't have time to waste; you are reaching the hour of decision: spiritual growth and depth, or shallowness due to busyness.

I don't believe God is against the building of churches, Bible schools, hospitals, or what ever may meet human need. He is set against ministers becoming addicted to building, the giving of themselves and all their time to these projects so that God is robbed of their best time and energy in the spiritual realm.

Which Temples Are of God And Which Are of Men?

The people of God must have a shelter from the elements in which to worship the Lord. Buildings are needed to meet the crushing problems of the poor, the addicted, the sick, the unwed mothers, etc. But there is a world of difference between a shelter and a showplace! Too many shepherds do not want a simple shelter; competition and ego demands a monument to self-achievement—something that makes a statement to others: "I am a mover and a shaker! I get things done! God deserves the best, and I'm the man to get it for Him."

True men of God build as a last resort. They build reluctantly, and they would rather die than overburden their dear sheep. They count the cost, and they build only as God provides. To strap God's people with monstrous debt is unconscionable and not of God. Yet Sunday after Sunday, pastors are forced to keep pressuring their congregations to sacrifice beyond their means to keep his big dream alive.

Solomon had promised to build God a house. God never intended that the project would get so out of hand the people would suffer because of it. Marvel, if you will, about his great building achievement; but as for me, I say he was far ahead of God. After his death, his son Rehoboam became king. Jeroboam, son of Nebat, led a tax reform committee on a royal mission to seek relief. "And Jeroboam and all the congregation of Israel came, and spake unto Rehoboam, saying, Thy father made our yoke grievous: now therefore make thou the grievous service of thy father, and his heavy yoke which he put upon us, lighter, and we will serve thee" (1 Kings 12:3,4).

Rehoboam refused and Jeroboam said, "To your tents, O Israel...So Israel rebelled against the house of David unto this day" (1 Kings 12:16,19).

No one can tell me our tender-hearted heavenly Father permitted a house to be built to His glory as a grievous burden on the backs of His beloved people. Especially for a temple, so soon rejected by God. In a few short years Solomon's temple was burned. "Our holy and our beautiful house, where our fathers praised thee, is burned up with fire: and all our pleasant things are laid waste" (Isaiah 64:11). All the building dreams of men soon fade into oblivion. They are so short lived.

Just like Israel of old, God's people are still crying out for relief, bending under the heavy yokes put on them by men whose building projects get so far ahead of God. Perhaps God gave some permission to build, but they themselves added and added, until God left them before they finished. They built a burden! Their people weary of hearing about the need for money continuously. And one of the greatest tragedies I can conceive is that a pastor lays a heavy yoke on a congregation, builds, then forsakes them, so he can find an easier place. Or, he threatens to leave them if they don't meet his demands. That happens all too often, and God keeps books on those men. They have no place in the ministry—they are heartless.

That which is of God simply meets the need and not fanciful, imagined, future needs. The real man of God, full of grace and mercy, will fight his board and elders to keep it only adequate. He will cut every bit of fat unmercifully and yearn for the day the shelter is finished so his people can get back to seeking God.

If it is of God, there will be no yoke, no grievous

burden, no hurting sheep, and no monstrous, unserviceable debt.

The Great Abomination in the Inner Court

"He said unto me: 'Hast thou seen this, O son of man? Turn thee yet again, and thou shalt see greater abominations than these.' And He brought me into the inner court of the house of Jehovah; and, behold at the door of the temple of Jehovah, between the porch and between the altar, there were about five and twenty men, their backs toward the temple of Jehovah, and their faces eastward; and they bowed themselves eastward to the sun" (Ezekiel 8:15,16 Spurrell).

What was this great abomination in the inner court of the house of Jehovah? Twenty-five prominent princes of Israel, standing between the porch and the altar—with their backs toward the altar. They were not blowing the trumpet in Zion, sanctifying a fast, calling a solemn assembly. They were not gathering the people to sanctify themselves before the Lord; they were not girding themselves and lamenting, lying all night in sackcloth; they were not howling because of sin and the withering of joy (Joel 1:13,14; 2:15-17).

Men of God who were called to "weep between the porch and the altar" had their backs to that altar and were facing the east. They were bowing down to the sun.

The twenty-five men symbolize the whole order of the priesthood as the seventy elders represented the laity. What terrible things Ezekiel saw going on behind closed doors. The seventy men of the ancestors of the house of Israel corrupting their minds and imaginations with idols "pictured upon the wall round about" (Ezekiel 8:10). This represents a laity who, by their actions, say, "The Lord seeth us not; the Lord hath forsaken the earth" (Ezekiel 8:12). Their minds had been totally corrupted; they practiced idolatry while continuing in the service of God's house.

But the greatest abominations of all were being practiced by the priesthood, the ministry. There they stood in the inner court, provoking God, not even understanding the gravity of their actions. Not a tear, not a single trumpet blast, not one lifting his voice in lamentation or repentance. They were looking to the sun—the god who gave them light by which they could fulfill the imaginations of their minds. This signifies the pursuit of power and dreams for a prosperous future. These were the twin features of sun worship.

Solomon, the world's most ambitious builder, said, "I have seen all the works that are done under the sun; and behold, all is vanity and vexation of spirit" (Ecclesiastes 1:14). After a lifetime facing the sun, building his dream, and laboring day after day, he ends up despising it all. "Then I looked on all the works that my hands had wrought, and on the labour that I had laboured to do: and, behold, all was vanity and vexation of spirit, and there was no profit under the sun" (Ecclesiastes 2:11).

I was once one of those priests in the inner court with my face in the wrong direction. I purchased 350 beautiful East Texas acres to build a center "for God's glory." I spent four years in construction; and I would finish one project, only to jump into another: A school, dormitories, gymnasium, old western village, hotel, swimming pool, playground, lakes—endless building. I stayed up late in the night beseeching God's help, crying to my supporters for money, and always fully convinced God was in every move I was making. My office was a plan shop, my counselors were builders and architects.

It was not ego, it was not ambition; it was the furious activity of a divided heart seeking release. I thought I was giving myself to human need, and hundreds of thousands of dollars were spent trying to scratch an itch I could not locate. I was too blind then to understand I was not really building in the proper realm. It was a realm of flesh—sincere, compassionate flesh.

The more I built, the less joy it brought me. I related to everything Solomon wrote, "It's all vanity—there is no profit to it!" One day the Spirit of God came upon me and clearly said, "Walk away from it all. Give it to another. Come, build my temple—get back to people." I have never regretted leaving that empty world of construction, planning, scheming, and the work of hands.

Not for a moment do I believe all ministers are caught up in the competitive spirit of outbuilding others. I've been in churches recently where God's glory was present, and the pastor and congregation were totally oblivious to what had been constructed. Their only concern was to meet the needs of the people, and they took no pride in their buildings. All was done with a view to simply provide a house of worship. Neither pastor nor congregation cared what others were doing; they stayed within the Holy Spirit's prescribed guidelines. I love preaching in those churches because of the sense of humility and reverence that prevails.

What I am prophesying against is the spirit of competition, the need to be bigger and better than others—to be the center of attraction. I decry the building of temples and institutions and projects by men of ambition, men no longer broken over the sight of starving sheep, men who lie and cry for money to carry on an endless building spree that has little to do with saving the lost. I denounce, in the name of the Lord, men whose public outcry for money is so obnoxious that the wicked mock and think of God's house as a den of thieves. The money appeals coming out of some ministry headquarters lately are an indignation to a holy

God. Some of them are outright lies, a barbarous crime in the eyes of the Lord. God loathes it; and He has promised to shut it all down. He said, "I will diminish them...I will diminish their ordinary food, and deliver them unto the will of them that hate them" (Ezekiel 16:27).

Ant Hills and Sand Castles

Jesus had one thing to say about temple building. His disciples came to Him to show Him the magnificent buildings of the temple. Jesus waved it all aside and said, "See all these things? Verily I say unto you, There shall not be left here one stone upon another, that shall not be thrown down" (Matthew 24:1,2).

God sees our temples and building projects as so many ant hills and sand castles. He could just as easily send His glory to fill a tent as a temple. I honestly believe God looks down on all our busy building activities, our running to and fro to erect things, as so many ants building ant hills; as children on the beach building sand castles—all of which could be washed away with one crashing wave of divine judgment.

It takes a real man of God to stand before his temple, or his institution, raise his hands to God, and cry out in humility, "Oh, God, I've built nothing but a sand castle! Time will decay it! The day will come when there will be nothing here but dust. Not one stone of these buildings will remain!"

How sad to think of men spending a lifetime building a dream, giving their very lifeblood to erect it, only to stand before God and hear, "I was not a bit interested! I didn't care! It meant nothing to Me!" I honestly don't believe our God is at all concerned about any of our temples or buildings. He simply tolerates them. Some projects He despises! He is more interested in building us a sure house, to fit us more perfectly into the heavenly building of which He is the chief cornerstone.

"Thus saith the Lord, The heaven is my throne, and the earth is my footstool: where is the house that ye build unto me? and where is the place of my rest? For all those things hath mine hand made, and all those things have been, saith the Lord: but to this man will I look, even to him that is poor and of a contrite spirit, and trembleth at my word" (Isaiah 66:1,2).

Oh, the grand delusions of men, and how quickly God deflates them all. He says, "It's all been done before! I'm not looking for builders but for contrite servants who tremble at My Word." Still, there are men of God who judge their worth by the size and value of their buildings. How sad!

That which appears to be God's blessing upon a man's constructions is by no means evidence of holiness or divine approval. Solomon built the world's greatest temple, while all along cleaving to strange women. He not only loved to build, he loved many women. He ended up a decrepit old man who could find pleasure in nothing. It is heartbreaking to read of a once great man of God so backslidden, he builds temples of doom, dedicated to the idols and gods of his heathen wives.

Noah Built an Ark

In a day of violence and God's impending wrath, what should a man of God be building? Noah built an ark!

"The earth also was corrupt before God, and the earth was filled with violence. And God said unto Noah, The end of all flesh is come before me; for the earth is filled with violence through them; and, behold, I will destroy them with the earth" (Genesis 6:11,13).

This holy man had a prophetic eye and he had heard God's call to prepare. He built the ark to the saving of his family. Oh, for more holy men of God in this day of violence and corruption who would give themselves wholly to the saving of the people of God. There should be a heartrending cry from our pulpits, from every television evangelist, of soon-coming judgment on this nation. We have far surpassed the violence of Noah's day, and God is going to shorten the days and pour out His wrath.

Contrast the preaching and project of Noah with what we are seeing today: recreation centers, tourist attractions for believers, multi-millions being spent for ridiculous projects—while the nation totters on the brink of judgment. If we only knew how close we are to the breaking forth of God's wrath and all its horrible tribulations, we would not be so wrapped up in material things. Men of God would not be wasting time building structures soon to burn.

The day before divine judgment falls, some will still be making their selfish plans; men of God will still be scurrying about looking for multiplied thousands of dollars to construct something to the glory of Jesus.

What makes all this such madness is that, with all this frantic building for God's glory, there is little or no corresponding sense of urgency about Christ's coming or judgment on sin. We call on the people to sacrifice, to give, to work—but we do not lead them into the full counsel of God's heart; we do not send them forth to get oil for their lamps; we do not warn them to trim their wicks; we do not shake them to awaken and go forth to meet the Bridegroom.

Preaching success and prosperity and endless material blessing to a generation about to be carried before the Judge of this earth is criminal. If preachers are not alarmed, if they are at ease, building, planting, buying, and selling—where will God's people end up? They will end up lounging on beds of ease, eating and drinking and making merry; building their own cieled houses; drinking their wines from silver goblets; living only for the pleasures of the hour. Zion is at ease because there is no trumpeter there. "Who is blind, but my servant? or deaf, as my messenger that I sent? Who is blind as he that is perfect, and blind as the Lord's servant? Seeing many things, but thou observest not; opening the ears, but he heareth not" (Isaiah 42:19,20).

Church Growth Cult

Whatever happened to "And the Lord added to the church daily such as should be saved" (Acts 2:47)?

The Catholics play bingo; evangelicals play the numbers. It makes me wonder if the message today is, God wants His church big, rather than holy.

Thank God for big churches. Jesus preached to the multitudes, also. There is nothing evil about big ministries. Thousands were added to the church at Pentecost, and growth is natural to a healthy body. But I see a caution light blinking from heaven's portals on this matter. Growth is now reduced to formulas, and carnal motives are creeping in. In a quest for big numbers, all kinds of compromises are being made. The count is becoming more important than the content. Men's egos are being stroked by the bigness of the parishes.

I find it appalling that some preachers today have set their goal for the biggest church in town, the nation, the world. There must be 2,000 "fastest growing churches in America." The goal is size, more than depth. Poor Gideon; he must have been terribly misled, sending back all those warriors who were not serious, not fully committed.

God, Give Us Men Who Will Do Their Works in Private!

Jesus' brethren prompted Him to undertake some great public work so that people would know God was with Him. They said to Him, "Go into Judea, that thy disciples also may see the works that thou doest" (John 7:3).

That is precisely the thinking of the flesh realm—"Do something that can be seen! Build something great! Do something magnificent—so the people may see how anointed and powerful you are."

Listen to the philosophy of the flesh. "For there is no man that doeth any thing in secret, and he himself seeketh to be known openly. If thou do these things, shew thyself to the world" (John 7:4).

No man of God on earth will admit he is building "to be known openly." Who will admit that by his great works he is "shewing himself openly to the world"?

But why is it that ministers build such gorgeous projects, then at the dedication, they call in as many reporters and cameramen as they can locate? Why do they want the whole nation to see and hear the stories of their achievement? If the goal is purely evangelism, only then can God truly bless it.

How true—the only man of God who is not in it for the glory is the man who does it "in private," away from the press. Christ's brothers were so right. No man—no exception to the rule. What is done so blatantly in public is a man seeking to be known! Read it!

Listen to the glowing description—see the gorgeous brochures—look at all the dignitaries on the platform—the magazine, newspaper, and TV reporters. Where, oh where can God find pastors and evangelists who will build only to meet the need; do it quickly, privately, get it all over, and stay always in the background, meek and humble?

Sadly, we will go on doing our works in public, seeking to be known, and showing ourselves openly to the world. Jesus said, "Therefore when thou doest thine alms, do not sound a trumpet before thee, as the hypocrites do in the synagogues and in the streets, that they may have glory of men. Verily I say unto you, They have their reward. But when thou doest alms, let not thy left hand know what thy right hand doeth: That thine alms may be in secret: and thy Father which seeth in secret himself shall reward thee openly" (Matthew 6:2-4).

The Matter of Circumcision

Moses was chosen by God to be a leader and a deliverer. On his way back to Egypt to obey his commission, the Lord intercepted him. It was an incredible encounter. "And it came to pass by the way in the inn, that the Lord met him, and sought to kill him" (Exodus 4:24).

Why would God want to kill a man He had just called and anointed to do a great work? We dare not overlook the significance of this awesome scene. Moses was in grave danger—God Himself was set to kill him. Why? Because Moses was about to undertake his great mandate with a disobedient heart. He knew how necessary it was to be in a covenant relationship with God before he made a single move. He had forgotten the matter of circumcision.

Zipporah, his wife, circumcised Gershom their first-born son. "Then she said, A bloody husband thou art" (Exodus 4:26). She could not have paid him a higher compliment because he was now under blood covenant, obedient, and prepared to fulfill his mission.

Circumcision lost its meaning unless those so marked "walked before him, blameless" (Genesis 17:1). It was the costly demand made by God of a man chosen to be a leader.

We are not to scorn the sign of circumcision even today under the New Covenant. As a work of salvation, it is worthless. As a "cutting off of the flesh," in circumcision made without hands, it is imperative. Paul never defamed such a circumcision (Galatians 5:12).

This has everything to do with the building of temples and projects. Most building projects are not under blood covenant, nor are the builders. No man of God has a right to break ground for any kind of building until his heart has been circumcised. Furthermore, God demands that all his people be circumcised of heart also. There can be no flesh involved. There can be no sin hidden in the life of the builder. What is born and built out of a divided heart is doomed, the glory of God will never fill that house—not unless or until the matter of circumcision is attended to.

What right does a pastor have to build a temple for a people who are not walking fully in holiness before God? He is only adding to their sin. A revival of righteousness must first cleanse the present house before another is erected.

Every structure built in the name of God without everyone involved having been circumcised is an act of disobedience. And if I were a pastor or evangelist who recently dedicated a sanctuary to God, I'd not give sleep to my eyes until the congregation came to "the hill of foreskins," and submitted to a wholesale heart circumcision. Meaning, a revival of holiness and the putting aside of all sin and evil. Every church needs that "one bloody encounter" with the holiness of God.

What Does It Have to Do With Repentance?

Here is the principle of righteousness by which all temples and projects may be judged to be right or wrong, of God or of self: What does it have to do with repentance?

John the Baptist's temple was the great outdoors, and he came preaching repentance. "He preached in the wilderness,...Repent ye" (Matthew 3:1,2). It was said of Christ, "He began to preach and to say, Repent" (Matthew 4:17).

How many ministers carefully look over every building, every item, and ask themselves, "What does this have to do with repentance? Is this necessary for the delivery of souls from iniquity?" When you see and hear of all the great new projects being constructed by pastors and evangelists, have you not wondered what it had to do with the saving of souls? Have you never asked, "Is this what God wants in this midnight hour with judgment about to fall?"

When you see the pictures of starving orphans around the world, how do you reconcile that horror with the fancy, expensive projects being built by pastors and evangelists that have nothing to do with evangelism or repentance? How can they throw millions of dollars into their toy dreams while the world starves and this nation rushes pell-mell to a holocaust? Why aren't they spending every dime on warning sinners to flee from the wrath of God? Why aren't they crying out, with tears, for national repentance? I know of only a few national television evangelists who do so! They are true prophets to this nation and I pray much for them. God help this nation when they are gone.

Jeremiah said of the squandering shepherds, "They have healed also the hurt of the daughter of my people slightly, saying, Peace, peace; when there is no peace. Were they ashamed when they had committed abomination? Nay, they were not at all ashamed, neither could they blush: therefore they shall fall among them that fall: at the time that I visit them they shall be cast down, saith the Lord" (Jeremiah 6:14,15).

Christians, wake up! How can any true lover of Jesus support these great abominations? You who send money to build buildings and projects that have nothing to do with repentance and revival are partakers in these men's sins. You, too, will be judged with them. In the name of all that is pure and righteous—stop! Not another dollar! They could not build their abominations if God's people had discernment and quit supporting them. Send all your giving to shepherds who preach righteousness and repentance.

Soon our blessed Lord will roar from the firmament and send terror into the hearts of these squanderers of God's money. I hear it ringing in my soul from the very throne of God, "The Lord will terrorize and cause to tremble all who have schemed and planned and constructed the dreams of flesh! It's all over! God has had enough! He will cut off their money supply and bankrupt them! One by one they will fall! Ichabod will be written over their doorposts! Their enemies will prevail over them. And God will shake out of His holy church all that is man-centered and nonessential!" God's holy Word backs this prophecy to the letter. "They are waxen fat, they shine: yea, they overpass the deeds of the wicked: they judge not the cause, the cause of the fatherless, yet they prosper; and the right of the needy do they not judge. Shall I not visit for these things? saith the Lord: shall not my soul be avenged on such a nation as this? A wonderful and horrible thing is committed in the land; The prophets prophesy falsely, and the priests bear rule by their means; and my people love to have it so: and what will ye do in the end thereof?" (Jeremiah 5:28-31).

Thank God, the BRANCH has come and He has built the true temple. He is the one appointed master builder. "Behold the man whose name is The BRANCH; and he shall grow up out of his place, and he shall build the temple of the Lord: Even he shall build the temple of the Lord; and he shall bear the glory, and shall sit and rule upon his throne; and he shall be a priest upon his throne: and the counsel of peace shall be between them both" (Zechariah 6:12,13).

Chapter 6
Pillow Prophets!

"O my people, they which led thee cause thee to err, and destroy the way of the paths" (Isaiah 3:12).

Ezekiel stood alone against all the false prophets of Israel. These prophets would have nothing to do with the message of righteousness and impending judgment. Instead, they prophesied an era of peace, ease, and prosperity.

Ezekiel 13 is the very word of Jehovah against preachers and prophets who accommodate people with flesh-pleasing words they said were from the Lord. Their words were designed to make God's people comfortable in the face of impending judgment.

In fact, they were not satisfied to prophesy good times ahead from their great houses and ivory beds of ease—they sought to provide a pillow for every elbow. "Woe to those who apply pillows unto all elbows..." (Ezekiel 13:18 Spurrell). "...Behold, I am against your pillows, wherewith ye entice souls..." (Ezekiel 13:20).

Ezekiel was horrified at the sight of prophets who had developed an art of making God's people comfortable. The Lord had said, "My people have set up idols in their hearts; they are brazenly setting up stumbling-blocks in iniquity; they are all estranged from me because of their idols" (Ezekiel 14:1-5).

The true word of the Lord was, "Jehovah says—eat your bread with trembling, and drink your water with grieving and fainting—and say unto the people, her land shall be emptied of its fullness, because of the violence—cities will be laid waste, the land made desolate—there shall be no more vain visions or flattering prophecies..." (Ezekiel 12:17-24).

While Ezekiel went about calling the people to humility and repentance, trying to prepare God's people for the soon coming judgments, these pillow prophets went about prophesying the dreams and imaginations of their own hearts. God had not spoken to them, even though they prefaced their predictions with, "Hear the Word of the Lord." God said, "I DID NOT SEND THEM: THEY DO NOT SPEAK FOR ME."

They carried with them fancy pillows to place under every elbow for all who flocked to hear their false prophecies. They placed handkerchiefs on the heads of every one of their disciples, a statement to others that meant, "Nothing but good times ahead. I see nothing ahead but peace and luxury." They walked among the poor and sick, with lace kerchiefs on their heads as a sign of their confidence in the message of the prophets of self-indulgence and comfort.

Ezekiel thundered the Word of God at them, as the masses congregated to hear their pleasant words. "You see for God's people a vision of prosperity, when there is no prosperity, saith the Lord Jehovah" (Ezekiel 13:16 Spurrell). "You follow after your own imagination—when actually you have seen nothing" (Ezekiel 13:3).

Jeremiah, a true prophet of God, stood before the house of the Lord and cried aloud, "This house shall be like Shiloh, and God will make this city a curse to all the nations of the earth" (Jeremiah 26:6).

The backslidden priests and the pillow prophets "took him, saying, Thou shalt surely die. Why hast thou prophesied in the name of the Lord, saying, This house shall be like Shiloh, and this city shall be desolate without an inhabitant?" (Jeremiah 26:8,9).

The pillow prophets incited the people against this "prophet of doom," saying, "Jeremiah is worthy to die for his prophecies." He would have been killed by those pillow prophets if the princes of the king's house had not delivered him from their zealous hand. "Then said the princes...unto the priests and prophets; This man is not worthy to die: for he hath spoken to us in the name of the Lord our God" (Jeremiah 26:16).

Jeremiah continued prophesying judgment, and the pillow prophets continued to mock him while they went about telling their own dreams and prophecies of peace and prosperity. Jeremiah challenged them saying, "The prophet which prophesieth of peace, when the word of the prophet shall come to pass, then shall the prophet be known, that the Lord hath truly sent him" (Jeremiah 28:9).

For a while Jeremiah sounded like a false prophet, while peace and prosperity continued. But suddenly Nebuchadnezzar and his brutal armies were at the door! Jerusalem was plundered! God's house became as Shiloh, and the people were taken captive. The pillow prophets were silenced and shamed.

The pillow prophets are still with us! They talk about the Word of God, about prophecy; and they salt their soothing messages with a lot of Scripture. But there is a falseness in what they preach. They are not preaching the Cross or holiness and separation. They make no demands on their followers. They seldom speak of sin and judgment. They abhor the very mention of suffering and pain. To them, the heroes of Hebrews were faithless cowards and penniless losers who were afraid to claim their rights. "Behold, I am against the prophets, saith the Lord, that use their tongues, and say, He saith. Behold, I am against them that prophesy false dreams, saith the Lord, and do tell them, and cause my people to err by their lies, and by their lightness; yet I sent them not, nor commanded them: therefore they shall not profit this people at all, saith the Lord" (Jeremiah 23:31,32).

Like the pillow prophets of Israel, their one supreme desire is to promote luxurious lifestyles and make people comfortable in their pursuit of the good life. They are not speaking for God. All they are doing is passing out pillows, one for every elbow of every follower. No wonder the crowds flock to sit under their message—it's painless. There is not the call of Christ to deny self and take up a cross. "Thus saith the Lord of hosts, Hearken not unto the words of the prophets that prophesy unto you: they make you vain: they speak a vision of their own heart, and not out of the mouth of the Lord. They say still unto them that despise me, The Lord hath said, Ye shall have peace; and they say unto every one that walketh after the imagination of his own heart, No evil shall come upon you" (Jeremiah 23:16,17).

Pillow Prophets Have Created the Laodicean Church

The prophets of comfort, ease, and prosperity have created the Laodicean church age referred to in Revelation 3, a lukewarm church going about speaking into being a constant increase in goods, riches, and all that the body could possibly need.

"Thou sayest, I am rich, and increased with goods, and have need of nothing" (Revelation 3:17). Do you know of teachers and believers today whose gospel features these very things? How clear can God's Word be on the subject? They were claiming with their mouths: riches, increases in goods, and the end of every pain and need. A people with no more needs—in need of nothing!

God said of them, "You don't know that you are wretched, and miserable, and poor, and blind, and naked" (Revelation 3:17). I find this to be utterly tragic, yet I see it everywhere I go now. These rich, but spiritually poor, approach me and ask, "Are you prospering?" Not, "Are you growing in the knowledge of Christ?" or "Are you seeking the face of God, denying self, and taking up His Cross?" They want to know if I have reached the place of needing nothing.

What sorrows my heart most about all this is that believers wrapped up in this cultic teaching are harder to reach with the gospel of surrender and sacrifice than those who have never heard of Christ. Their teachers have culled out of God's Word an avalanche of Scriptures to "prove" their message—but they cull out only the blessings and not the curses.

A rich, in-need-of-nothing people eventually becomes a lukewarm people. They become wretched, blind to their own spiritual poverty. God points them out as the victims of a special kind of misery.

I receive many letters now from revived believers who write, "Thank God for delivering me out of that false gospel. I was blinded by it. The teachers seemed so sincere; the need to be somebody, so deep in me. I wanted success; I wanted to get ahead. But it ended in total despair. Now I am back to worship, back to the Lordship of Christ, back to simple faith in God's mercy and grace."

I say again, unequivocally, that pillow prophets have been responsible for the creation of the present-day Laodicean spirit. They are blinding believers; they are taking their eyes off the need to rid their lives of sin and coziness with the world. They are not entering into the Spirit's call to weep and howl between the porch and the altar—they have tasted the fruit of success and prosperity, and they have poisoned the sheep with the same perverted gospel. Some would rather see the world prosper than be purified. Zephaniah said to them, "And it shall come to pass at that time, that I will search Jerusalem with candles, and punish the men that are settled on their lees: that say in their heart, The Lord will not do good, neither will he do evil" (Zephaniah 1:12).

I scan the messages of the pillow prophets, hoping to find a gospel I can relate to—some ground of fellowship. But it's been all in vain. I hear them boast that prosperity is the message of this last hour, and I want to run to the secret closet and say to my heavenly Father, "Could it be we are incurably blind? How can men of God make this their message?" There is no burden, no blood, no self-denial, no sacrifice, no taking up His Cross, no cry against sin and iniquity. There is no call to holiness and separation, no call to repentance and humility, no word of brokenness, conviction, intercession, or burden for the damned.

What is the difference between pillow prophets and Jehovah's true prophets? The preacher or parishioner who doesn't know the difference is on dangerous ground. With so many going about gathering huge followings, it is imperative to have Holy Ghost discernment. The confused prophets must be exposed by truth. Most of them look and sound like sincere, Bible-loving men of God. But the Lord has given His people infallible tests to prove what is true and what is false. We are to test every man and every message—by the whole Word of God.

Let me bring to your attention three characteristics of a true prophet of God.

1. A true prophet of God is consumed with a vision of the Lord Jesus Christ!

He has been so overwhelmed, so mastered by that glorious vision, he can speak of nothing else. He preaches the whole counsel of God—but as it relates to Christ.

God said of the false prophets, "Woe unto the deceiving prophets who follow after their own imaginations; THEY HAVE SEEN NOTHING" (Ezekiel 13:3).

Yet, of Moses it was said, "By faith he forsook Egypt, not fearing the wrath of the king; for he endured, AS SEEING HIM WHO IS INVISIBLE" (Hebrews 11:27).

Jesus said of Abraham, "Abraham rejoiced to SEE my day: and HE SAW IT, and was glad" (John 8:56).

Stephen had a glorious vision of Him. "And he said, Behold, I SEE the heavens opened, AND THE SON OF MAN standing on the right hand of God" (Acts 7:55).

Ananias said to Paul, "The God of our fathers hath chosen thee, that thou shouldest know his will, AND SEE THAT JUST ONE, and shouldest hear the voice of his mouth" (Acts 22:14).

To His own disciples, Jesus said, "In a little while the world will see me no more, but YOU WILL SEE ME" (John 14:19).

The one thing every one of these men of God had in common was their life-controlling vision of Christ the Lord. Christ was the great and only cause in their life. They saw Him through the eye of faith.

Moses willingly forsook the ease and prosperity of Egypt to suffer privation in a wilderness, because he had been mastered by a vision of Christ. Nothing else mattered now, not even his dream of becoming a great deliverer. He saw beyond all human ambition. He was weaned from all that was earthly because he had seen Christ. He could endure anything, for nothing on earth could compare with what his spiritual eyes beheld.

Abraham became totally detached from this world and willingly became a foreigner on earth, for his eyes were fixed on a city whose builder and maker was God. But best of all, he had seen a vision of Christ on His throne in that holy city. Never again would he settle for things temporal or earthly. His faith was built upon his continual vision of Christ. He rejoiced and was glad, for he had eyes for the invisible, the eternal Christ!

The moment Paul saw Him, everything else on earth became dung to him. The very moment Christ was revealed in him, he determined to know nothing else among men but his Lord. He gladly endured hardships, shipwreck, stoning, beatings, privations, imprisonment; none of these things moved him because he gloried in his vision of the Lord.

Any man of God who is tied to this earth or the things of earth has seen nothing. If he had a vision of Christ, if he was in constant union with Christ, he could preach of nothing else. He would stand before the crowds, proclaiming, "I count it all loss—it's all dung! It is Christ and Him alone. He is all; He fills all things. He is my very life."

Like Isaiah, the true man of God who sees the Lord high and lifted up will fall on his face and weep over his sins and the sins of God's people. Then he will be purged and go forth in the power of his awesome vision to preach Christ.

God warned Israel, "The prophets are like foxes...." In other words, some have no single eye focused on Christ alone, but they have eyes filled with covetousness. They spoil the vine, taking the best for themselves. They go their own way, feeding their own egos!

These self-seeking prophets claimed to have heard from God. Theirs, they claimed, was a prophetic word directly from heaven. "They say, Jehovah saith, when

Jehovah hath not sent them; and they caused others to hope that their word would be verified" (Ezekiel 13:6).

The multitudes of God's people who run about to hear only soothing messages need to take a second, honest look at what they are hearing and believing. "Have ye not seen a deceiving vision and spoken a lying divination when you said, Jehovah saith, whereas I have not spoken" (Ezekiel 13:7). "They have seduced my people, saying, Peace, when there was no peace" (Ezekiel 13:10). Their message was, "God told me all is well. No trouble ahead. Good times! No trial or tribulation. God's desire is that all be happy, prosperous and at ease." Jehovah calls that deception!

I don't think ministers are taking seriously enough the tragedy of preaching the wrong message. How dare we preach peace and endless good times to a nation and a people on the brink of judgment! "Is not my word like as a fire? saith the Lord; and like a hammer that breaketh the rock in pieces?" (Jeremiah 23:29).

Israel's sin was about to explode in unbelievable fires of divine wrath. Ezekiel did not want to preach such a disturbing message, especially to a people who had heaped to themselves pillow prophets who went about telling God's people that all was well.

Listen to what God was trying to say to His people. "Therefore thus saith the Lord Jehovah: like as the wood of the vine amongst the trees of the forest, which I have given unto the fire to devour, so have I given the inhabitants of Jerusalem. And I will set my face against them: from one fire shall they escape that another fire may devour them....I have set my face against them....I will make this land desolate, because they have trespassed a trespass, saith the Lord Jehovah" (Ezekiel 15:6-8 Spurrell).

The people rejected the true Word of God. The masses ran off after their favorite teachers to hear the deceptive message—"God is not that kind of God. He desires only the best for us all. Great peace and good times lay ahead. Don't listen to the old prophets of doom. God told me right from His throne room that the best is yet to come."

I ask you, what will those pillow prophets do when God begins to judge the sins of this nation and cut off its bread and its fullness? Think of the unprepared multitudes of sincere Christians who should be repenting of lukewarmness, who should be weeping because of compromise and covetousness, who should be forsaking all rather than accumulating.

Thank God, the Holy Spirit is raising up a holy people who are sick of all the self-centered ministries, and their cry is, "We would see Jesus." The man-centered gospel cannot last much longer. A time of purging is ahead. We are heading into refining fires. While the covetous lounge on their beds of ease and comfort themselves with luxuries, a remnant will break away and go out seeking the Bridegroom. Christ is going to reveal Himself to the humble, the poor in spirit, and the true Word of the Lord will flow forth with unction and power. Union with Christ will become the pearl of great price.

2. A true prophet of God preaches and practices self-denial.

Compare this with what the pillow prophets focus on! God said of them, "They pollute me among my people for handfuls of barley, and for morsels of bread...they lie to my people" (Ezekiel 13:19). A modern translation is, "These pillow prophets have money on their minds. It has made liars of them."

Here is the full picture of a pillow prophet. He lets his imagination run wild. He operates on the idea that prosperity will last forever. He builds on dreams and schemes. To do it, he needs money—lots of it. His need for money becomes the focus of his ministry. He ends up telling lies to God's people to get it. Then he pollutes it all by saying, "God told me." Micah the prophet said, "The heads thereof judge for reward, and the priests thereof teach for hire, and the prophets thereof divine for money: yet will they lean upon the Lord, and say, Is not the Lord among us? None evil can come upon us" (Micah 3:11).

The message of Jesus Christ is painfully blunt: **Deny yourself and take up your cross**. "Then said Jesus unto his disciples, If any man will come after me, let him deny himself, and take up his cross, and follow me" (Matthew 16:24).

Self-denial—what a foreign-sounding concept in this day of self-pampering and ease. The pillow prophets have rejected it flat out. Self-denial is the giving up and forsaking of all and everything that hinders the constant presence of Christ.

There is no merit in self-denial. We are saved and secured by grace alone. It is not to be entered into to earn benefits from God. But self-denial removes hindrances to constant communion with Christ. Paul said, "I bring my body under, and bring it under subjection: lest that by any means, when I have preached to others, I myself should be a castaway" (1 Corinthians 9:27).

We are not bringing our bodies under control; our passions and appetites are not under subjection. Sensuous television programs now whet the fleshly appetites among Christians for pornography. Lust is nearly out of control, even in the ministry. I hear of ministers who spend hours viewing X-rated movies and cassettes.

Multitudes of God's people, including preachers of the gospel, waste precious hours lounging before the TV idol. Like Lot, our minds are getting vexed by the things we see and hear.

Food is becoming the narcotic of believers. We don't need cocaine or alcohol—we have a legalized sedative: food. Never in all my ministry have I seen so many Christians with appetites out of control.

The deepest truth about self-denial goes beyond giving up material things. You can sell your TV, shun all erotic sights and sounds, and bring all appetites under control, and still not have denied self.

What Christ is calling for is a kind of devotion to Himself that expels everything in the heart that hinders. It is a commitment to becoming absolutely nothing before God and man. It is being able to say with Paul, "I no longer live—it is Christ living in me."

The world must lose its charm to us. We must die to all self-ambition, to all attachments to earthly things, until we can honestly say, "I am dead to this world and all it represents. I no longer live."

Physically alive, yes! But I must die to all that hinders my vision and love for Christ. Whatever it is—it must go. Lust? Self-made plans? Bitterness, grudges? Recognition, self-esteem? I must die to it all. I must bring it all to the Cross and execute self-judgment.

Why is it that Christians who are about to die become so detached from the world and material and physical things? Because eternity is in view. It all pales in comparison to the joy ahead. Why can't we live like that all the time? Why not keep our minds fixed on Christ at all times?

3. A true prophet of God has a holy boldness against sin—he never whitewashes evil!

"Son of man, cause Jerusalem to know her abominations" (Ezekiel 16:2). "Cry aloud, spare not, lift up thy voice like a trumpet, and shew my people their transgression, and the house of Jacob their sins" (Isaiah 58:1).

The pillow prophets have no foundation of holiness upon which to build. Ezekiel said, "Their foundation thereof shall be discovered..." (Ezekiel 13:14).

The pillow prophets were building walls with untempered mortar and painting the flaws over with whitewash. Worst of all, their message and manner "grieved the hearts of the righteous because of their falsehoods" (Ezekiel 13:22).

True prophets, sent by God, always show God's people their sins. Their one desire is to turn believers away from their wicked ways. "And the Lord hath sent unto you all his servants the prophets, rising early and sending them; but ye have not hearkened, nor inclined your ear to hear. They said, Turn ye again now every one from his evil way, and from the evil of your doings, and dwell in the land that the Lord hath given unto you and to your fathers for ever and ever" (Jeremiah 25:4,5).

Pillow prophets "strengthened the hands of the wicked." God accused them of damning souls by ignoring sin. It grieved God that compromising children of God were being encouraged rather than exposed. Lightness about sin only confirmed them in their compromising. "I have not sent these prophets, yet they ran: I have not spoken to them, yet they prophesied. But if they had stood in my counsel, and had caused my people to hear my words, then they should have turned them from their evil way, and from the evil of their doings. I have heard what the prophets said, that prophesy lies in my name, saying, I have dreamed, I have dreamed. How long shall this be in the heart of the prophets that prophesy lies? Yea, they are prophets of the deceit of their own heart" (Jeremiah 23:21,22,25,26).

Every preacher of peace and prosperity should study the Lamentations of Jeremiah and repent for teaching such vanity and foolishness, instead of preaching repentance and holiness. Jeremiah said, "Thy prophets have seen vain and foolish things for thee: and they have not discovered thine iniquity, to turn away thy captivity; but have seen for thee false burdens and causes of banishment" (Lamentations 2:14).

Where God sent judgment on Israel for their sinful ways, the pillow prophets and backslidden priests were the first to look out for their own safety. "My priests and mine elders gave up the ghost in the city, while they sought their meat to relieve their souls" (Lamentations 1:19).

Instead of peace and prosperity, "God afflicted His chosen people for their horrible iniquities" (Lamentations 1:5). The tabernacle, all palaces, all homes, were burned with fire. The gates and walls were pulled down. The elders sat on the ground throwing dust on their heads. Children and babies wept for food. "They that did feed delicately are desolate in the streets: they that were brought up in scarlet embrace dunghills" (Lamentations 4:5). Women ate their own children. "The hands of the pitiful women have boiled their own children: they were their meat in the destruction of the daughters of my people" (Lamentations 4:10). God's people held their heads down to the ground. There was mourning and lamentations everywhere. God poured out His fury just as His true prophets said He would. Then we read, "The law is no more; her prophets also find no vision from the Lord" (Lamentations 2:9). Judgment silenced all preaching of prosperity and sent the pillow prophets scurrying just to save themselves. God said the enemy came to destroy Jerusalem, "For the sins of her prophets, and the iniquities of her priests" (Lamentations 4:13).

God will not let any minister of the gospel grieve or trouble His chosen and devoted ones without His express permission. But neither will He permit prophets of ease to call evil good—and pamper backslidden Christians who need to repent.

Certainly we are called to proclaim the gospel of grace, mercy, and pardon. But the man of God is also commanded, "Cry aloud, spare not, lift up thy voice like a trumpet, and show the people their transgression" (Isaiah 58:1).

Could it be we can't lift up a holy standard because of corruption in our own hearts? Have our own sins robbed us of holy boldness? Do we wink at the sins of others because of besetting sins in our hearts?

Do you know of a man of God who boldly thunders against sin? Does his message ring, not of legalism, but of deep personal purity? Then run to his feet—sit under his message, for he has the truth that will set you free. He is the true prophet of God, and he makes all other prophets tremble and fear. The pillow prophets despise him because he walks with truth in the inward parts.

Seek out a man of God who makes Christ real! One who makes you sit up and take notice that he has been with Jesus. One who convicts you for wasting time and for becoming earthly minded. One who will point a finger in your face, discern sin, and cry out, "Thou art the man." He is the one who truly loves you and looks out for your soul.

The pillow prophets are building their huge walls. They look very successful and blessed. But Jehovah says, "Your walls shall fall. I will bring it all down with my stormy wind. I will demolish your wall and level it to the ground" (Ezekiel 13:11-14).

God has told us that in these last days our young men shall see visions. Not of success, of prosperity, or of great achievements. There will be but one vision for all—CHRIST!

Chapter 7

Blow the Trumpet in Zion — For The Day of the Lord Has Come

"Blow the trumpet in Zion, and sound an alarm in my holy mountain: let all the inhabitants of the land tremble: for the day of the Lord cometh, for it is nigh at hand" (Joel 2:1).

O Zion, holy people of God, awake to the sound of the trumpet, for the day of the Lord is near, and our King cometh in glory with His armies to set up His kingdom.

O ye slumbering saints of the Most High God, shake yourselves, and put away the evil of your doings, and put on the whole armor of God; for the enemies of God have determined to war against the Lord and His saints. "A day of darkness is coming, and of gloominess, a day of clouds and thick darkness...a great people and a strong; there hath not been ever the like, neither shall be any more after it, even to the years of many generations. A fire devoureth before them.... Before their face the people shall be much pained: all faces shall gather blackness" (Joel 2:2-6).

Zion, have you not yet heard that "the earth shall quake before them; the heavens shall tremble: the sun and the moon shall be dark, and the stars shall withdraw their shining" (Joel 2:10)?

Seeing then that very soon the very elements are going to melt with fervent heat, why do the people of the Lord lounge on beds of ease and go on carelessly, eating and drinking and making merry? Have you not yet heard, O Zion, the trumpet sounding? Have you become so blinded by prosperity, so deafened by the lusts and cares of this world that you cannot hear? Can you not discern the times; know ye not the day of the Lord is at the very door? Is this a time to be at ease, to give all your time and energy to your own interests? Will you go days on end and not seek His face? Will you keep on forgetting Him who called you out of bondage? Will you neglect His Word, His house, His secret closet? Will you comfort yourself by saying, "He is not coming! Judgment is not near! I will relax, enjoy my life and pleasures, and go to be with Him when I have finished serving my own desires"?

The Spirit saith, Blow the trumpet in Zion and call my people to "turn to me with all their hearts, and with fasting, and with weeping, and with mourning: And rend your hearts, and not your garments; and turn unto the Lord your God; for he is gracious and merciful, slow to anger, and of great kindness, and repenteth him of the evil. Who knoweth if he will return and repent, and leave a blessing behind him?" (Joel 2:12-14). He is even now "setting a mark upon the foreheads of the men that sigh and that cry for all the abominations that be done in the midst of them" (Ezekiel 9:4).

"Blow the trumpet in Zion, sanctify a fast, call a solemn assembly: gather the congregation, assemble the elders, gather the children,...let the bridegroom go forth out of his chamber, and the bride out of her closet" (Joel 2:15,16).

Where are the priests of the Lord who should be weeping between the porch and the altar? Where are those prophets who have been awakened and who cry aloud, "Spare thy people, O Lord" (Joel 2:17)? The priests are asleep! "And there is none that calleth upon thy name, that stirreth up himself to take hold of thee: for thou hast hid thy face from us, and hast consumed us, because of our iniquities" (Isaiah 64:7). Already Christ the Bridegroom has left His celestial chamber, and He has set out to meet His bride. And even now the Spirit cries to the bride to awaken and go out to meet Him, whom her soul loveth. Should not the shepherds be on their faces before God, weeping, confessing their sins and the sins of God's people? Should not the priests of the Lord be stirring the bride? My God, how blind Your shepherds have become. While the armies of Satan align themselves to do battle with heaven, while the armies and chariots of God march in rank to the final conflict, the shepherds play. "Son of man, prophesy against the shepherds of Israel, prophesy, and say unto them, Thus saith the Lord God unto the shepherds: Woe be to the shepherds of Israel that do feed themselves! Should not the shepherds feed the flocks? Ye eat the fat, and ye clothe you with the wool, ye kill them that are fed: but ye feed not the flock" (Ezekiel 34:2,3). They turn on their soft beds, feeding themselves on the fat of the sheep. They gather their male sheep to the ball fields. They go forth hunting and fishing, but not for men. They love to party, to socialize, to relax before their idols. "And they were scattered, because there is no shepherd: and they became meat to all the beasts of the field, when they were scattered. My sheep wandered through all the mountains, and upon every high hill: yea, my flock was scattered upon all the face of the earth, and none did search or seek after them" (Ezekiel 34:5,6).

O blind shepherds of Zion, you have been called to gather God's people to a solemn assembly—not to foolish fun and games! "Son of man, prophesy, and say, Thus saith the Lord; Say, A sword, a sword is sharpened, and also furbished. It is sharpened to make a sore slaughter; it is furbished that it may glitter: should we then make mirth?" (Ezekiel 21:9,10). You have been commanded by the Lord of hosts to set your face to the ground in humility, brokenness, and repentance. Do you lament, O man of God? Are you ashamed, O ye husbandmen of Zion? Awake ye drinkers of wine, for the enemy has come upon the land and ye know it not. There shall be heard the "voice of the howling of the shepherds; for their glory is spoiled" (Zechariah 11:3).

The vine lays waste; the seed is rotting under the clod; the cankerworms have eaten the fields; and no one mourns! Every man looks to his own interest; the love of many grows cold; and joy is withering from the sons of God. It is because there is no shepherd in the pulpit who is alarmed; none who has heard the sound of Zion's trumpet; none who have purged themselves from all iniquity and who proclaim the day of the Lord with power! "Her prophets are light and treacherous persons: her priests have polluted the sanctuary, they have done violence to the law" (Zephaniah 3:4).

He could have healed the backslidings of this nation if the Lord's shepherds had been awake and watching. But the watchmen's eyes have grown heavy with slumber, and the priests refuse to call mightily upon His name. His anger could have been turned away, had there been ministers in the house of the Lord who were on their faces, calling on heaven to forgive and heal the people.

Why do the children forsake the ways of the Lord? Why do the young people cozy to the daughter of Babylon and run with the wicked? Why are they so angry, so faithless, so set in their worldly ways? It is because there is no clear and solemn word from the pulpits of the land. Ministers, burdened with their own doubts and sins, stand before the powers of darkness, cowering, for they have lost their spiritual authority.

A holy remnant of faithful shepherds is still in the land. They weep for the flock; they grieve over the sins of God's people; they have returned to the Lord with all their might—yet, they are a despised few. Many prophets have become bags of wind, and God's people love to have it so.

The congregation of Zion is spoiled! The day of the Lord is at hand; the land is perplexed; there is desolation and destruction threatening on all sides—yet, the Lord's people do not take it to heart. The church is in the valley of indecision; the Spirit has gone forth to awaken and stir the sleeping—yet, there is no fear of God before their eyes. Approaching judgment? Not until they see the end of their favorite television series. Not until the last dregs of pleasure have been wrung out. Not until the easy life ebbs and withers. Not until all fleshly desires and ambitions have been fulfilled. "Do not interrupt us, O God," they seem to be saying, "for the Lord's coming or sudden judgment would deny us of all that our hearts are set upon."

O ye backslidden people of Zion, will you never return to the Lord with all your hearts and put away the adulteries, the fornications, the pleasure madness?

God Will Overthrow!

Our King is coming to Zion to rule with a rod of iron. If His people will not humble themselves, confess and forsake their sins, He will come suddenly to His temple to execute judgment: mercy and grace upon all who crown Him Lord and King; peace and rest and joy to all who seek Him with all their hearts, minds, souls, and strength; green pastures, living waters, restoration to all the people of God who turn to Him from all that is of this world: its ways, its things, its spirit, and its seduction. "As a shepherd seeketh out his flock in the day that he is among his sheep that are scattered; so will I seek out my sheep, and will deliver them out of all places where they have been scattered in the cloudy and dark day. I will feed them in a good pasture, and upon the high mountains of Israel shall their fold be: there shall they lie in a good fold, and in a fat pasture shall they feed upon the mountains of Israel" (Ezekiel 34:12,14).

But quick judgment and sorrow upon all who shut their ears and close their minds to the trumpet sounding in Zion! He will overthrow the seducers of mankind. He will overthrow the hypocrites and the cold-hearted. The lukewarm will He spew out of His mouth. He will release to Satan all who hold the truth in unrighteousness. He will give over to a reprobate mind all who knew God but glorify Him not as God, but become conceited fools who worship the creature more than the Creator. He will overthrow the lazy shepherds who have fed themselves and not their flocks. "Therefore ye shepherds, hear the word of the Lord: As I live, saith the Lord God, surely because my flock became a prey, and my flock became meat to every beast of the field, because there was no shepherd, neither did my shepherds search for my flock, but the shepherds fed themselves, and fed not my flock; therefore, O ye shepherds, hear the word of the Lord: Thus saith the Lord God: Behold, I am against the shepherds; and I will require my flock at their hand, and cause them to cease from feeding the flock; neither shall the shepherds feed themselves any more; for I will deliver my flock from their mouth, that they may not be meat for them" (Ezekiel 34:7-10). He will overthrow all who changed the truth of God into a lie. It is a day of dread release! Millions who scoffed at the trumpet sound and who carried on in their foolishness and apathy will be given up to the wrath to come. "The sun and the moon shall be darkened, and the stars shall withdraw their shining. The Lord also shall roar out of Zion, and utter his voice from Jerusalem; and the heavens and the earth shall shake: but the Lord will be the hope of his people, and the strength of the children of Israel" (Joel 3:15,16).

The Redeemer Has Come!

"The redeemer shall come to Zion, and unto them that turn from transgression, saith the Lord" (Isaiah 59:20). "Arise and shine; for thy light is come, and the glory of the Lord is risen upon thee" (Isaiah 60:1). Darkness shall cover the earth, and gross darkness the people; but the Lord shall arise upon thee, and his glory shall be upon thee. The people of the Lord, the overcoming bridehood, shall lift up their eyes and sing, "Our King cometh. He cometh to save us! To nurse us! To bring us into the abundance of His holy city!"

And the overcomers will flow together; they shall be as one and be manifest to the world as the body of Christ on earth. But the body is soon to be united with its Head. The Head of this glorious body is the Redeemer of Zion, and He will appear suddenly in His temple to set up His throne. Their hearts shall not fear who long for His coming. They shall show forth His praises till He comes. They will adore Him until the moment of resurrection. Their days of mourning shall pass. The glory of the Lord shall ever be upon them, and as they see the day approaching, their hearts shall leap for joy. When He breaks through the dark clouds of judgment, the redeemed remnant will shout mightily—for they will suddenly stand before His glorious presence; they will look lovingly upon His majestic face; and they will fall before Him with singing and with rejoicing, proclaiming, "We endured for the joy that awaited us! This is our joy! Christ, King of Glory! Hosanna to Him who brought us out of great judgments, who preserved us in the fires, who redeemed us with a high and mighty hand."

Where once there was fear of death and destruction, there will now be only the excellency of His eternal joy. He will plant our feet in a glorious land, and He Himself will be our sanctuary. No more will we be hated; no more pain-burdened; no more concern or worry about any tomorrows—for we will be home with Him! We will drink the milk of heaven and eat the food of angels. We will not look back at all; the fears and forebodings will be forever gone.

Why do we fear dying? Why do we hold to this fleeting life so tenaciously? Why do we dread the leap into eternity? Who would exchange the city of gold and the eternal pleasures of His kingdom for the paltry, decaying, corrupted existence here on earth?

Resurrection Life

Did our Lord not tell us that He is the resurrection and the life? And that whosoever liveth and believeth in Him should never die, but have everlasting life? That everlasting life is to be enjoyed right now! The Lord seeks to bring His overcoming remnant into THE POWER OF AN ENDLESS LIFE.

It is greater than Pentecostal power. Greater than power to heal the sick, cast out devils, and to perform great works. It is greater than witnessing power, and even greater than power to raise the dead. Soon, very soon, those powers will no longer be needed because a new world will be born. A world is coming where there is no limited measure of the Spirit. There will be no need to cast out devils, heal the sick, or raise the dead. No witnesses will be needed then. It is an eternal world where everlasting life will flow endlessly in all who are redeemed. We can only speculate what it will be like to be in the full power and glory of eternal life.

God seeks to bring His holy remnant into the power of eternal life, even now. Not that we will not die, but that the power of everlasting life will be so appropriated in this life—there will be a full and complete severing from the world and its claims. God wants a free people, a remnant totally detached from all that is earthly and of time. It is possible to move into a resurrection realm that places us beyond time, beyond the thinking of this world, beyond the bondage of health, security, and death itself.

There is freedom in appropriating the power of endless life. To live with an eye fixed in eternity, focused on the throne of God, is to live without fear of what men can do to this human body. To live in a resurrected state of mind is to hold lightly to all that is in and of this world.

Is Jesus Christ more to His people than life itself? Yes—O yes—He is to us life everlasting! Cry it aloud, O saints of God; tell it to the world, the flesh, and the devil: "I will never die! I do not belong to this lost and dying world! I am even now, in Christ, an eternal being. My spirit will ever live with Him, and He will restore to me a glorious new body in His very own image." Is that not the greatest power God can give mankind—to make him an eternal being, a never-dying soul who will live forever in His presence? The life I will experience in eternity even now flows in me from God's throne. I have the earnest of that inheritance right now.

I can look down on this old, sin-cursed world and rejoice, "O world of wickedness and habitation of devils—you have no claim or hold on me! I have been released from your power. Even the grave in your dust cannot keep me imprisoned. I am even now endued from on high with an endless life, the life of God that has no beginning and no end!"

Get hold on eternal life, overcoming remnant! The life you now experience in the flesh is but a vapor that will soon vanish and be gone. Everlasting life flows from God's very throne, and it is also a fruit the redeemed will eat forever from the Tree of Life. But God seeks to reveal to us that it is possible to eat of that fruit now, in the Spirit, by faith. What unspeakable joy to be secluded with Him in the secret closet, and for hours drink of that fountain of everlasting life and eat of the fruit of the Tree of Life. You can come out of that prayer chamber already in heavenly places in Christ Jesus. The world loses its charm. The heart is weaned from all that was once held dear. The affections and longings are transformed to the heavenly kingdom, to the resurrection realm.

Hungering Hearts— Take Your Fill!

The overcoming remnant will hunger and thirst more and more in the final days before destruction. The Holy Spirit will create in Christ's bride an overwhelming desire for holiness, purity, and revelation. Here and there, throughout the land, the deep hungerings and thirstings of the righteous can be seen. Radical separations from the world and all its idols and pleasures are taking place. The cry is for a spirit of wisdom and revelation in the knowledge of Christ. Material things are losing their value to this bridehood. Their hearts are being wooed by the Spirit to a life of prayer and brokenness before the throne. Selfish desires, self-centered plans are being abandoned, and the perfect will of God is all that matters now. The man-realm of success, ambition, and promotion has been dealt a death-blow, and the glory of God has become supreme. There is the sound of adoration and worship, and the enthroning of Christ and the yielding to His lordship.

In these final days before the holocaust, the blessed Savior is preparing a feast of good things; not the beggarly elements of this world and the foolish materialism being sought by the undiscerning, but the blessings and joys of heaven itself. The overcoming remnant can face any furnace of fire with fully satisfied, restful hearts.

Sound the TRUMPET IN ZION—God has a secured remnant, washed in Christ's Blood, clothed with spotless garments, separated unto the King of Glory, with burning lamps held high, going out to meet the Bridegroom in the power of an endless life! Drink to the full, saints of God—drink of the fountain of everlasting life!

"Come Out of Her, My People"

"Come out of her, my people, that ye be not partakers of her sins, and that ye receive not of her plagues" (Revelation 18:4).

Come out of the sleeping, dead churches. Come out of the covetous, prosperity-minded cults. Come out of the lukewarm, socializing congregations who have lost the glory of the Lord. Come out of the compromising, sin-laden, liberal temples. Come out of the Mary-worshipping Catholic church. Come out of any and all churches and groups where there is no Holy Ghost fire, no smiting conviction, no hunger for holiness. Come out of the legalistic churches and fellowships that preach salvation by works. "Flee out of the midst of Babylon, and deliver every man his soul: be not cut off in her iniquity; for this is the time of the Lord's vengeance; he will render unto her a recompence. Babylon hath been a golden cup in the Lord's hand, that made all the earth drunken: the nations have drunken of her wine; therefore the nations are mad. Babylon is suddenly fallen and destroyed: howl for her; take balm for her pain, if so be she may be healed" (Jeremiah 51:6-8).

Come out of the teachings that encourage lust for money, fame, and success. Come out of all the man-centered religious institutions that are twice dead and plucked up by the roots. "My people, go ye out of the midst of her, and deliver ye every man his soul from the fierce anger of the Lord" (Jeremiah 51:45).

Come out and forsake the false prophets whose eyes are on the gold and the glory. Come out and forsake any minister or evangelist who puts you at ease in Zion and who comforts Christians with false security. "Depart ye, depart ye, go ye out from thence, touch no unclean thing; go ye out of the midst of her; be ye clean, that bear the vessels of the Lord" (Isaiah 52:11).

"For her sins have reached unto heaven, and God hath remembered her iniquities" (Revelation 18:5). Whose sins? The sins of the backslidden, lukewarm church and the corporate sins of a nation whose cup of iniquity is full. How dare we believe that God has not seen our incurable wickedness! The men of Nineveh and Sodom cry out for justice. They are our accusers. Nineveh repented at one sermon—America rejected an avalanche of gospel calls and warnings. Sodom had no gospel; it had no armies of preachers; nor was its airwaves flooded with warnings of impending judgment. As with Sodom, as with Nineveh, as with Jerusalem and Judah, our sins have reached into heaven and God has set His judgments. They are all gone, and now we stand at His bar of judgment.

Who will awaken, heed the Lord's call to come out and separate, and cleanse themselves from all the iniquities of the church and society? Do not do as Israel did and think the days of judgment are far off. "Son of man, behold, they of the house of Israel say, The vision that he seeth is for many days to come, and he prophesieth of the times that are far off. Therefore say unto them, Thus saith the Lord God: There shall none of my words be prolonged any more, but the word which I have spoken shall be done, saith the Lord" (Ezekiel 12:27,28).

Words of Comfort for Zion—God's Holy Remnant

"Zion shall be redeemed with justice, and her converts with righteousness. And the strong shall be as tow, and his work as a spark, and they shall both burn together, and none shall quench them" (Isaiah 1:27,31).

"Cry aloud and shout, thou inhabitant of Zion; for great in the midst of thee is the Holy One of Israel" (Isaiah 12:6).

"Strengthen ye the weak hands, and confirm the feeble knees. Say to them that are of a fearful heart, Be strong, fear not: behold, your God will come with vengeance, with the recompence of God; he will come and save you. And a highway shall be there, and a way, and it shall be called the way of holiness; the unclean shall not pass over it; but it shall be for the redeemed: the wayfaring men, yea fools, shall not err therein. No lion shall be there, nor shall any ravenous beast go up thereon; they shall not be found there; but the redeemed shall walk there: and the ransomed of Jehovah shall return, and come with singing unto Zion; and everlasting joy shall be upon their heads: they shall obtain gladness and joy, and sorrow and sighing shall flee away" (Isaiah 35:3,4,8-10).

"The voice of one saying, Cry. And one said, What shall

I cry? All flesh is grass, and all the goodliness thereof is as the flower of the fields. The grass withereth, the flower fadeth, because the breath of Jehovah bloweth upon it; surely the people is grass. The grass withereth, the flower fadeth; but the word of our God shall stand for ever. O thou that tellest good tidings to Zion, get thee up on a high mountain; O thou that tellest good tidings to Jerusalem, lift up thy voice with strength; lift it up, be not afraid; say unto the cities of Judah, Behold your God! Behold, the Lord Jehovah will come as a mighty one, and his arm will rule for him: Behold, his reward is with him, and his recompence before him. He will feed his flock like a shepherd, he will gather the lambs in his arm, and carry them in his bosom, and will gently lead those that have their young" (Isaiah 40:6-11).

"For Jehovah hath comforted Zion; he hath comforted all her waste places, and hath made her wilderness like Eden, and her desert like the garden of Jehovah; joy and gladness shall be found therein, thanksgiving, and the voice of melody. My righteousness is near, my salvation is gone forth, and mine arms shall judge the peoples; the isles shall wait for me, and on mine arm shall they trust. Lift up your eyes to the heavens, and look upon the earth beneath; for the heavens shall vanish away like smoke, and the earth shall wax old like a garment; and they that dwell therein shall die in like manner: but my salvation shall be for ever, and my righteousness shall not be abolished" (Isaiah 51:3,5,6).

"How beautiful upon the mountains are the feet of him that bringeth good tidings, that publisheth peace, that bringeth good tidings of good, that publisheth salvation, that saith unto Zion, Thy God reigneth!" (Isaiah 52:7).

"The Spirit of the Lord Jehovah is upon me; because

Jehovah hath anointed me to preach good tidings unto the meek; he hath sent me to bind up the brokenhearted, to proclaim liberty to the captives, and the opening of the prison to them that are bound; to proclaim the year of Jehovah's favor, and the day of vengeance of our God; to comfort all that mourn; to appoint unto them that mourn in Zion, to give unto them a garland for ashes, the oil of joy for mourning, the garment of praise for the spirit of heaviness; that they may be called trees of righteousness, the planting of Jehovah, that he may be glorified" (Isaiah 61:1-3).

"Set up a standard toward Zion: flee for safety, stay not; for I will bring evil from the north, and a great destruction" (Jeremiah 4:6).

"And Jehovah will roar from Zion, and utter his voice from Jerusalem; and the heavens and the earth shall shake: but Jehovah will be a refuge unto his people, and a stronghold to the children of Israel" (Joel 3:16).

"But in mount Zion there shall be those that escape, and it shall be holy; and the house of Jacob shall possess their possessions" (Obadiah 1:17).